ISI
WALKS

C000066339

Warne Gerrard Guides for Walkers

Walks for Motorists Series

CHESHIRE WALKS
CHILTERNS WALKS
        Northern
        Southern
COUNTY OF AVON WALKS
COUNTY OF DURHAM WALKS
DARTMOOR WALKS
DERBYSHIRE WALKS
        Northern
        Southern
COTSWOLD WALKS
        Northern
        Southern
DORSET WALKS
EXMOOR WALKS
FAMILY WALKS IN MIDLAND COUNTIES
FURTHER CHESHIRE WALKS
HAMPSHIRE AND THE NEW FOREST WALKS
JERSEY WALKS
LAKE DISTRICT WALKS
        Central
        Northern
        Western
GREEN LONDON WALKS (both circular and cross country)
ISLE OF WIGHT WALKS
KENT WALKS
LONDON COUNTRYSIDE WALKS
        North West
        North East
        South West
        South East
LOTHIAN AND SOUTH EAST BORDERS WALKS
MIDLAND WALKS
NORTHUMBERLAND WALKS
NORTH YORK MOORS WALKS
        North and East
        West and South
PEAK DISTRICT WALKS
PENDLESIDE AND BRONTE COUNTRY WALKS
SEVERN VALLEY WALKS
SNOWDONIA WALKS Northern
SOUTH DEVON WALKS
SOUTH DOWNS WALKS
WYE VALLEY WALKS
YORKSHIRE DALES WALKS
FURTHER DALES WALKS

Long Distance and Cross Country Walks

WALKING THE PENNINE WAY
RAMBLES IN THE DALES

Warne Gerrard Guides for Walkers

ISLE OF WIGHT
WALKS FOR MOTORISTS

R. G. McInnes

30 circular walks
with sketch maps by
F. Rodney Fraser

FREDERICK WARNE

Published by
Frederick Warne (Publishers) Ltd
40 Bedford Square
London WC1B 3HE

I would like to acknowledge the help of Mr E. Leal and Mr T. Slade who provided information about diversions and checked the maps for errors. I would also like to thank my stepfather Dr E.F. Laidlaw for his invaluable assistance.

The photograph on the front cover is of The Needles. It was taken by Keith W. Terry and is reproduced by courtesy of the Isle of Wight Tourist Board. The photograph on the back cover is of Sandown Bay and Culver Cliff and was taken by N. Davis.

Publishers' Note

While every care has been taken in the compilation of this book, the publishers cannot accept responsibility for any inaccuracies. Things may have changed since the book was published; paths are sometimes diverted, a concrete bridge may replace a wooden one, stiles disappear. Please let the publishers know if you discover anything like this on your way.

The length of each walk in this book is given in miles and kilometres, but within the text Imperial measurements are quoted. It is useful to bear the following approximations in mind: 5 miles = 8 kilometres, $\frac{1}{2}$ mile = 805 metres, 1 metre = 39.4 inches.

ISBN 0 7232 2805 1

Phototypset by Tradespools Ltd., Frome, Somerset
Printed by Galava Printing Co. Ltd., Nelson, Lancashire

Contents

ISLE OF WIGHT

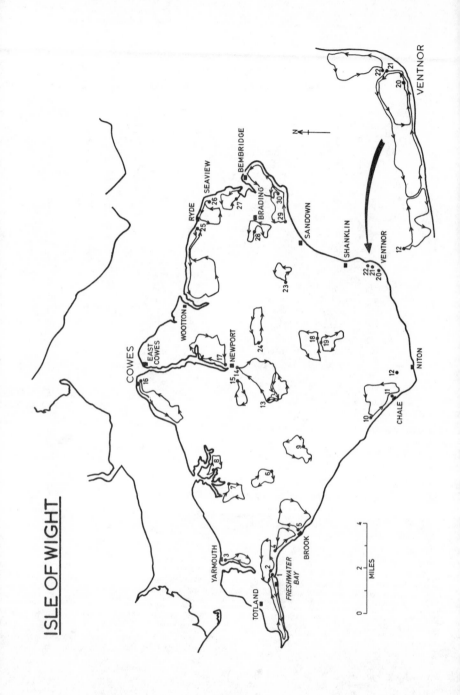

Introduction

The Isle of Wight has been alternatively described as 'the Garden of England' and 'an England in miniature'. Both these descriptions are accurate for they summarize the beauty and wide variety of scenery to be found within this small area. The continually changing landscape of high cliffs, chalk downland, meadows and estuary, together with the dramatic Undercliff make the Island ideal walking country and this is enhanced by an excellent footpath network over all parts.

The Isle of Wight County Council have over the years provided perhaps the finest system of signposting and waymarking to be found in any region. Nearly every path has a sign designating the parish in which the path lies, the footpath number and its destination. An Ordnance Survey map will provide additional information, and in greater detail than sketch maps can show. Sheet no 196 of the 1:50,000 series covers the whole Island.

The history and other aspects of the Isle of Wight are well documented but the following introduction to the Island and its scenery may well give the prospective walker ideas on which part of the Island he may wish to visit as well as briefly outlining the general background to the area.

Each of the thirty walks described in the book follows a circular route of between three and eight miles and commences at an easily located parking place. Particular care should be taken to avoid damage to gates and walls and to follow the Country Code:

Guard against all risks of fire
Fasten all gates
Keep dogs under proper control
Keep to the paths across farmland
Avoid damaging fences, hedges and walls
Leave no litter—take it home
Safeguard water supplies
Protect wildlife, wild plants and trees
Go carefully on country roads
Respect the life of the countryside

By virtue of the Island's size none of the routes is over particularly extensive wild or isolated countryside and farms and villages will be close to all paths. However, sensible clothes and footwear are advised as some of the downs and coastal walks become extremely

7

exposed in adverse conditions.

In addition to the description of each walk a number of the ancient buildings or items of particular interest are described *en route* and it is hoped these will give added enjoyment during the course of each walk.

Until as recently as 1800 Islanders rarely ventured on a journey across the Solent without first making a will, and likewise it was only the occasional trader or traveller who crossed to the Isle of Wight. The narrow strip of water which separates the Island from mainland England formed a natural barrier against any early development, and it was not until regular ferry services were established in the 1850s that the Island began to expand as a resort.

The introduction of a ferry service was one of a number of factors that encouraged rich families to visit the Isle of Wight. A further encouragement was a claim by an eminent physician that the Undercliff had a particularly beneficial climate. The Island became fashionable after both Queen Victoria and Lord Tennyson had settled there, and the opening of a railway line between Ryde and Ventnor gave the final impetus required to encourage large scale expansion.

Engravings from the Victorian era show how the Island scenery was greatly admired by the early visitors, and today it is the variety of scenery, as much as the warm climate, that brings well over a million holidaymakers across the Solent each summer. Within an area of 155 square miles there are high chalk downs, open farmlands, forests, salt-marshes and mudflats; whilst the geological structure has resulted in such landforms as the coastal stacks known as the Needles, the tumbled mass of the Undercliff, and the coloured sands of Alum Bay.

The Island itself is lozenge-shaped, $23\frac{1}{2}$ miles long and $13\frac{3}{4}$ miles wide. The long east-west axis is clearly marked by the ridge of downs which extend from Culver Cliff to the Needles, whilst the north-south axis runs from Cowes to St Catherine's Point. The principal river, the Medina, follows a northward course along this line and divides the Island into two distinct regions: the East Wight, with three-quarters of the 110,000 population, and the West Wight, with the remaining quarter. The imbalance was brought about by the opening of the railway which linked the east coast resorts and this, together with their superior natural locations, resulted in a more rapid development in the East Wight.

Historically, however, the villages of the West Wight achieved much greater importance in the past when both Newtown and Yarmouth were major ports and trading centres. Successive attacks by the French in the Middle Ages, and the silting up of the Newtown and West Yar rivers, led to their gradual decline after two centuries of prosperity. From that time the capital town of Newport, which was sited at a bridging point of the River Medina, became the Island's chief port.

Newport also suffered attacks by the French, and nearby Carisbrooke Castle provided refuge for residents in times of trouble. The castle achieved some importance at the close of the Civil War when Charles I was held prisoner there prior to his execution in 1649. Today the castle is open to the public and together with Osborne House (a former residence of Queen Victoria) they provide the two most popular venues for visitors. Apart from Carisbrooke and the smaller castle at Yarmouth, there are other historic buildings representing all periods of English architecture. The earliest remains of buildings are the Roman villas of Brading and Newport, and it has been suggested that the Island with its mild climate was favoured by retired army officers. Medieval styles are well exhibited in the village churches whilst Jacobean and Georgian styles are best seen in the numerous small country houses and farms. There is of course a predominance of Victorian architecture with marine villas and large country houses forming the bulk of the south-east coast development. Most of the larger properties have been converted into holiday accommodation, and many can be accurately dated by their pseudo-Italianate style which became popular after the completion of Osborne House.

Modern development is most evident on the outskirts of the East Wight towns, and although there has been some expansion of the villages in the West Wight this remains the least populated part of the Island. The wildest region is the 'back of the Wight', or that length of coast between Blackgang and Freshwater. Here there are high sandstone cliffs, which are cut by deep ravines (or chines as they are known locally), and windswept farmlands that are flanked by the chalk downs. The southern slopes provide shelter for a line of picturesque villages, and through these runs the inland road to Newport. Many of the stone and thatched cottages in such rural communities now form holiday accommodation or retirement homes, whilst formerly they housed farmworkers, fishermen, and smugglers who worked the surrounding land and coastal waters. The rocks of the 'back of the Wight', the Bay of Chale and Atherfield Point in particular, have been the site of over 150 wrecks since 1750, and there are many tales of wrecks and smuggling relating to that area.

That part of the West Wight north of the downs is also predominantly rural. Here the high cliffs are replaced by estuaries and salterns which form habitats for a rich variety of wildlife. Newtown Nature Reserve on the north-west coast is well known to ornithologists, and the creeks and harbours are also popular with yachtsmen.

Yarmouth is the principal village of the West Wight and is a leading sailing centre, with its harbour full of local and international craft during 'the season'. Both Yarmouth, and Bembridge in the East Wight, are of course overshadowed by Cowes as sailing venues. Cowes Week is Europe's most important sailing event, and it is held in early August. Yachts from all over the world take part in the major races which have been a feature of the town since the early nineteenth century following the foundation of the Royal Yacht Squadron.

As well as being a recreational centre, Cowes (and East Cowes) on the east bank of the Medina is the location of the Island's principal industries, with ship-building, services related to yachting, and the hovercraft industry, being of chief importance.

As with any small island the Isle of Wight has several present-day problems. These include a steady increase in cross-Solent traffic resulting in congestion in the summer months, a very high proportion of retired residents, relatively poor job opportunities, and a distinct lack of trade for many businesses during six or seven months of the year. Despite these problems it is evident that there is much to offer both the resident and the visitor in the form of recreation, peace and natural beauty.

Landscape

Although the Island's scenery has changed dramatically over the last 150 years, the purchase of large areas of downland and coast by the National Trust, and the introduction of planning legislation have minimized the detrimental effects of a massive increase in population. The Island's remarkable scenery is related to its geological history and the chalk downs of the Central and South Wight give it much of its character.

The backbone of the Island is the chalk ridge which extends east-west across the county and which is broken only by the rivers Medina, East Yar and West Yar. The central ridge varies in height from 250 to 700 ft above sea level and provides an element of shelter for the inland villages and farmlands as well as forming a natural viewpoint in both northerly and southerly directions.

The second downland mass lies in the Island's south-east corner where St Boniface and Shanklin Downs drop steeply to the sea from a height of almost 800 ft. It is between these downs and the sea that much of the Island's tourist trade is concentrated, the development taking advantage of the sunny, southern aspect.

Whilst the downlands provide far-reaching views of the inland scenery, it is at the coast, where rock is under constant erosion by the sea, that its geology is most evident in the role of providing the structure and landscape of the Island. The 60 miles of coastline can be divided into five distinct lengths, namely the north-east coast from East Cowes to Culver Cliff, the south-east coast which forms Sandown Bay, the Undercliff of the South Wight, the south-west coast or 'back of the Wight', and the north-west coast from the Needles to Cowes. An examination of the scenery of each of these lengths of coast gives a clear understanding of how a wide variation in rock type can cause the formation of different coastal features and without doubt it is the rapid variation of coastal landforms that is the Isle of Wight's attraction.

The north-east coastal belt between East Cowes and Ryde provides the least majestic scenery as it lacks a cliff line. However, the coastline is not developed for the most part, and the heavy clay soils are thickly covered by oakwoods which are broken only by the creeks of Wootton and Kings Quay. Wootton Creek, the larger of the two inlets, is a beautiful stretch of water which penetrates inland for some two miles and is fed by a stream from the downs to the south. These creeks and inlets are typical of the Solent's island and mainland shores, and form havens for wildlife as well as offering recreational opportunities in an unspoilt environment.

To the east of Wootton Creek the land undulates in a hill and vale landscape with the town of Ryde occupying a prominent position nearby. It is the Ryde Sands that are the town's chief attraction and at low tide the sea retreats almost a mile to expose the beaches which were the key to the town's development when bathing became fashionable during the last century.

East of Ryde the land slopes gently to the flood plain of the East Yar, a meandering stream which has cut a valley through the central chalk ridge and which enters the sea at Brading Harbour. By carving through the chalk the River Yar has almost marooned the easternmost part of the chalk ridge which constitutes the headland of Culver Cliff. Apart from its geological importance, Culver is of great scenic interest with bright sands and clays adjoining the chalk to the north and an equally colourful sequence to the south.

Although the chalk has been undercut and eroded by the sea causing the formation of a wavecut platform on the foreshore, the softer neighbouring clays and sands of Whitecliff Bay and Sandown Bay have been eroded at a greater rate with the result that distinct bays have formed on both sides of the headland. Rounding Culver Cliff in a southerly direction one enters the wide scoop of Sandown Bay where the ferruginous sands known as Redcliff contrast vividly with the whiteness of the chalk, and where the strata can be seen dipping down on both sides of the bay away from the core of the Sandown anticlinal fold.

Following the shore line to the southern extremity of Sandown Bay the land rises again with deep orange-brown sandstone cliffs towering high above the wide sandy beaches. Here the cliffs have been incised by fast flowing streams to form chines or ravines which lead down to the sea. The chines of Shanklin and Luccombe are classic examples of this landform. To the south of Luccombe the unstable cliffs have been subjected to constant erosion resulting in a landslip topography with much terracing and slumping of soil and larger sections of cliff.

The south coast of the Isle of Wight from Bonchurch east of Ventnor to Blackgang, some seven miles to the west, forms the slipped terrace of land known as the Undercliff. As its name suggests the Undercliff forms a bench below the main cliff from which it slipped and consists of a belt of fallen strata between $\frac{1}{4}$ and $\frac{1}{2}$ mile in width. The general character of the scenery is of a high cliff wall varying between 100 and 150 ft, at the base of which lies the fallen material. The most distinctive feature of the cliff is the banding in the upper part which has been formed by differential weathering of the hard and soft layers of rock. The result is a rugged and craggy appearance to the scenery which is emphasized by a luxuriant growth of vegetation encouraged by the warm climate and sheltered position.

Apart from the cliff itself which occupies a prominent position along the south coast it is the downlands and coves which complete the scenic picture. The coast is rugged with the many small coves backed by steep cliffs whilst the beach material is coarse shingle with some sand. All along this coast there is evidence of the instability of the ground and large boulders of derived materials from the upper cliffs are to be found at different levels between the top of the Undercliff and the beaches. Behind the Undercliff are the high chalk downs of St Boniface and St Catherine's and it is their seaward face from which the Undercliff has fallen away.

In order to appreciate the magnitude of land movements along the Undercliff it is necessary to follow the old coastal road from St Lawrence to Niton and then proceed to the terminus of this road at Windy Corner. Formerly the road continued along the base of the Undercliff to Blackgang $\frac{3}{4}$ mile to the west but this road was carried away by a huge landslide in 1928. Looking at the waste of tumbled boulders and slumped soil which now extends from the cliffs down to the sea over many acres, it is easy to appreciate the havoc that can be caused by the percolation of rain water through the porous chalk to the underlying, slippery Gault Clay.

Less than $\frac{1}{2}$ mile south of the cliffs of Windy Corner lies St Catherine's, the Island's most southerly point; the lighthouse, which is one of the most powerful in Europe, warns ships of the dangerous coast to the east and west. The western end of the Undercliff at Blackgang marks the beginning of the Island's south-west coast or the 'back of the Wight'.

The finest view of the 15-mile coast of the 'back of the Wight' is obtained from the viewpoint at Gore, above Blackgang. Immediately below is Blackgang village with its deep and cavernous chine whilst in the mid-distance Atherfield Point and its notorious ledge project out to sea, and then far beyond are the chalk cliffs of Freshwater, the Needles rocks and the coast of Dorset. In many respects this part of the Island's coast is like the Sandown area on account of a similar arrangement of strata and the re-appearance of erosion features such as the chines, of which Blackgang, Whale, Shepherds, Grange and Chilton are notable. Further west at the village of Brook the cliffs reach their lowest point rarely exceeding 100 ft, but from there they rise rapidly with the oncoming of the chalk at Afton. (The chalk re-appears at this instance because the central ridge meets the coast at Compton Bay.) The rise from clays and sands to more resistant chalk causes a high arching of the cliffs at Afton Down but this height is quickly lost with a rapid westward descent into the perfectly circular hollow of Freshwater Bay. This bay, which has been hollowed by the pounding of south-westerly gales on a line of weakness in the chalk, contains some fine sea stacks on its eastern side whilst a stone's throw inland across a narrow causeway are the headwaters of the West Yar. Immediately to the west of Freshwater Bay rise Tennyson Down and Main Bench whose 480 ft cliffs form a textbook example of a chalk headland.

The best views of the Needles rocks and Alum Bay are obtained by boat, and excursions from Yarmouth which take visitors around the headland to the high overhanging cliffs of Scratchells Bay are popular. The cliffs of Alum Bay itself curve northwards from the chalk in parallel, near vertical bands of colours ranging from red and orange to green, yellow and white with the strata changing gradually from a vertical to a horizontal position at Headon Hill. The coloured sands of Alum Bay are separated from the heatherclad Headon Hill by a shallow chine which allows access to the beach. However, the beach does not provide the best overall impression of the sands and the seascape to the north; a short walk along the promontary of chalk to the west or an easy climb to the top of Headon Hill is more worthwhile. From the summit of Headon Hill it is a matter of only a few hundred yards across the deepest part of the Solent channel to the curving shingle spit of Hurst Castle, and to the east and west the views are equally extensive with the Island's north-west coast on the one hand and the Needles rocks and headland on the other.

Although the rocks occupying the whole of the northern half of the Island tend to be clays and sands with some limestones, there are considerable variations in the height of land above sea level with a decrease in height to the east. From Headon Hill the cliffs lose height steadily past Totland and Colwell until there is a complete loss of cliffline west of Yarmouth. As the name suggests this port lies at the mouth of the West Yar river on its eastern bank and is situated on a causeway which leads eastwards between flood plains and the sea to higher land by Ningwood village.

East of Yarmouth at Cranmore the coastal scenery is clayey with heavy overgrowth of rough vegetation along the cliff edges where landslips are a regular occurrence in the winter. Whilst a short distance beyond at the hamlet of Newtown the coast is one of mudflats and salterns which are protected from the winter storms by two long spits extending to the west and the east. From Newtown eastwards the coastal scenery is variable with marsh and mudflats at Thorness and then a low cliff rapidly rising to over 100 ft at Gurnard near Cowes. Like the Cranmore cliffs this part of the north coast is subject to much land movement and after heavy rain some sections of the cliffs degenerate into slurries of brown oozing clay which cuts a swathe through the bracken and gorse on its way to the beach.

From Gurnard to Cowes the cliff line is lost by the construction of Cowes Promenade. Here a low beach suggests an original cliff line of perhaps 10 ft behind which is a gently rising hill that is now largely covered by residential development. The circular tour of the coast is completed on reaching the western shore of the River Medina which separates the towns of Cowes and East Cowes.

It is clear from a description of the Island's coast that variety in its structure, scenery and local colour is the key to its popularity and few islands can offer such a constantly changing landscape as each mile of the circular coastal road is travelled. Perhaps also the relationship between geology and scenery is more evident here than in many parts of Britain on account of the short distances involved and the obvious similarities between the scenery at such locations as Alum Bay and Whitecliff Bay or Sandown Bay and Brook Bay where the same geological horizons span the Island from east to west.

It is from the central downs that the true rural character of the Island can be confirmed, with the sand and clay soils offering delightful variations in the colour of the ploughed fields, and the forests, woods and downlands providing a backcloth in varying shades of green. It is hard to believe that the population of the Isle of Wight is in excess of 100,000 when one looks down over the most densely populated North and East Wight. From the downs above Brading the major development blends admirably with the landscape, villages shelter in the valleys, and parallel hedgerows are the only indication of busy roads.

Although there is a lack of any expanse of fresh water within the Isle of Wight there are many areas of marshland and salterns, as in any region where rivers flow through low lying plains to the sea. The most extensive marshlands are at Newtown where many fingerlike creeks penetrate for up to two miles inland. Other areas of marsh are to be found at the mouth of the Western Yar, a river which originates at Freshwater and follows a wide and shallow path to the sea at Yarmouth. The East Yar by contrast has a longer course. From its origins as a stream in the southern downs it turns north-east through a gap that it has cut in the chalk ridge and then widens out into a broad flood plain at Brading. Between Brading and the sea this river follows a meandering course and is subject to extreme flooding when heavy rain falls in its catchment area. The Island's principal river is the Medina which runs due north from the downs behind Niton and enters the sea at Cowes. This river is navigable for barge traffic between Cowes and Newport but quickly narrows to a small stream at Shide two miles to the south.

For the most part it is the scenery and bathing potential that attract visitors to the Isle of Wight. However, this has not always been the case. Following the acclaim given to the climate of the Ventnor area by Sir James Clark in 1830, there was a large influx of gentry and ladies from all parts of the country who came to benefit from the long hours of sunshine and the bracing sea air. The three resorts of the South Wight, Sandown, Shanklin and Ventnor, are renowned for their climate. These conditions are accounted for by their southern aspect together with the central position of the Island along England's south coast away from the influences of the east and west coasts. Another factor is the suntrap effect of a sheltered position beneath the central downs and the Undercliff.

As with mainland England it is the south-westerly winds which blow for over half the year with the 'back of the Wight' taking the brunt of the storms. Evidence of the strong winds can be seen in the hedges and trees which bow steeply away from the prevailing direction. The Island's warmest months are July and August with the mean monthly temperature of 62°F being exceeded on many occasions during the daytime. The coldest months are January and February but the presence of the sea tends to have a warming influence on the winter temperatures with the result that snow rarely falls in any quantity.

As in most coastal locations rainfall is higher and the Island, with an average of 28 inches receives more rain than East Anglia but substantially less than the west coast of England and this should be borne in mind for spring and autumn holidays. Thus the climate of the Isle of Wight can be summarized as being warm summers with high temperatures, mild winters and a moderate rainfall.

Walk 1   Freshwater to the Needles

6½ miles (10.5 km)

This walk covers the high chalk downland at the western end of the Island. From Freshwater Bay the route climbs steadily to the summit of Tennyson Down before providing a nearly level walk to the Needles headland. The return route is for the most part a gentle downward gradient making a total distance for the walk of 6½ miles.

The starting point is the public car park on the landward side of the road at Freshwater Bay opposite the sea wall.

On emerging from the car park cross the road and turn right past the Albion Hotel and after 100 yards turn left by the public conveniences. Walk up the narrow lane for 200 yards and on emerging at the foot of the down bear right up the hill to the Tennyson Monument. Follow the path parallel to the cliff edge (keeping well clear in windy weather) as it rises some 350 ft in ¾ mile. Pause near the summit and look back over the alcove of Freshwater Bay and beyond to the clay and sand cliffs of Compton Bay and Hanover Point.

The cliffs at the summit of Tennyson Down are some 450 ft high and consist of chalk which has been compressed during the Alpine Mountain Building Phase and is as a result particularly resistant to erosion. Many species of seabird have been recorded on these cliffs and guillemots, razorbills, several species of gull, birds of prey and members of the crow family will be encountered.

Tennyson Down is named after Alfred Lord Tennyson the Victorian poet who lived at Farringford House (now a hotel). Tennyson regularly walked this down while reciting and composing poetry and with his dark cloak, wide brimmed hat and dark beard was no doubt an impressive figure. His Gothic-style mansion can be seen in its parkland setting ¼ mile to the north.

From the Tennyson Monument continue straight on westwards down the hill and then up onto High Down which leads to the cliffs overlooking the Needles rocks. After 1¾ miles the path bends sharply to the right downhill to join the road that leads from Alum Bay to the Needles. The land to the west was formerly a defence establishment where a rocket was developed in the fifties and early sixties. More recently the land was acquired by the National Trust and access is now unrestricted, enabling the walker to view the magnificent flint-banded chalk cliffs and arched cave at Scratchells Bay. The bay was a particularly popular viewpoint in early

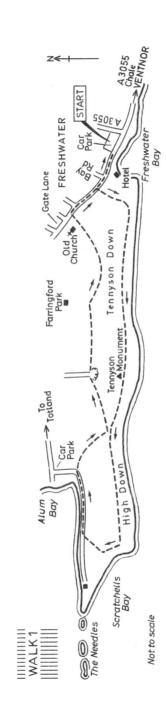

WALK 1

N

The Needles

Alum Bay

To Totland

Car Park

High Down

Scratchell's Bay

Not to scale

Tennyson Monument

Tennyson Down

Farringford Park

Old Church

Gate Lane

FRESHWATER

Bay Rd

Car Park

START

Hotel

Freshwater Bay

A 3055

A 3055
Chale
VENTNOR

Victorian times and was well illustrated by George Brannon and other early engravers. The Needles headland was the location of early wireless transmissions by Marconi as was Knowles Farm at Niton, at the southern tip of the Island.

Looking down on the Needles from the cliff top it will be noted that there is a gap between the first and second rock. This site was originally occupied by a tall stack known at Lot's Wife which was 120 ft high. This pinnacle collapsed in 1764 with such a noise that the rumble of falling stone was reputedly heard on the mainland.

Return to the path and descend onto the road and continue east (inland) along the road for ½ mile. At the point where the road bends sharply to the left continue on the footpath straight ahead. A diversion on down the road at this point leads to Alum Bay. Access to the beach can be gained by either taking the chairlift or descending the long flight of steps down the chine.

The sands are spectacular here because earth movements have tilted the strata from a horizontal to near vertical position. The resulting thin bands of different coloured strata contrast magnificently against the white cliffs. After viewing Alum Bay return up the road to the footpath to commence the return journey to Freshwater Bay. The route follows the northern slope of Tennyson Down roughly along the 300 ft contour. After 1 mile of straight walking the route bears right to join the outward path and immediately bears to the left again down the lower slopes. Continue for 600 yards and at the point where the path opens into the entrance to a small chalk quarry carry straight across (following the sign up the bank on the side of the access lane). The next 1½ miles are through picturesque downland with glimpses of small farms and country houses among open fields to the north. After passing a second quarry the path divides. The left turn leads towards Freshwater village and circuits the grounds of Farringford House. Carry straight on at this point to emerge onto the Freshwater to Freshwater Bay road (known as Gate Lane) just below the old thatched church. This is one of the few thatched churches in the country and despite the misleading date-stone the building was erected as late as 1908 on land donated by the Tennyson family.

Turn right down the road which leads to Freshwater Bay. The large house on the right known as Dimbola was the residence of Julia Margaret Cameron the pioneer Victorian photographer and close friend of Lord Tennyson. Mrs Cameron's style of photography, the 'faded' appearance that characterized her portraits, is particularly popular at present and many local people were subjects for her camera.

On reaching Freshwater Bay cross the road opposite the Albion Hotel to reach the car park.

Walk 2   Freshwater to Afton

5 miles (8 km)

Without doubt the walks over the high chalk downs in the West
Wight provide some of the most spectacular routes to be found
locally. This walk starts in the gap in the downs formed by the River
Yar at Freshwater Bay and the path then rises up to the summit of
Afton Down eastwards. The return route runs north, then west over
downs and farmland, before following the Yar Valley back to the
starting point. Apart from the rise up to and down from the downs
the walking is easy and covers a total of nearly 5 miles.

The starting point is the large car park in Freshwater Bay
opposite the public open space behind the sea wall and close to the
Albion Hotel.

Turn left out of the car park and walk up the road past the junction
of Afton Road and on up the A3055 Military Road for 150 yards.
Turn left and up the gravelled Southdown Road. Cross this road
and walk uphill past the golf club. About 200 yards further on turn
left and then almost immediately right to continue eastwards along
the north side of Afton Down. After a short distance a track bears off
to the right over the down towards Compton Bay but carry on ahead
at this point. Continue east for a mile and on reaching a small chalk
quarry turn left and follow a high hedge and field boundary due
north down to the B3399 Freshwater to Newport Road.

The next section of the walk leads over rich and extensive
farmlands interspersed by fine farm buildings and small manor-
houses. The town of Yarmouth lies to the north-east with the
farming communities of Thorley, Wellow and Ningwood forming a
straggling line of development along the inland road to the north.

Cross the road and enter the field opposite turning left by a small
copse after 400 yards. To the left can be seen East Afton Farm. After
350 yards pass a track which leads to the farm and carry on until
Wilmingham Lane is reached. Cross the lane and enter the field
straight ahead and continue due west until the path reaches a quiet
lane. Turn right along the lane and after 100 yards stop by the old
stone bridge at The Causeway over the estuary of the River Yar. A
small lodge beside the bridge lies close to the old railway line and
there is an attractive walk to Yarmouth along this route. Many
species of wading bird and marsh plant are to be found in this
locality.

Turn left opposite the lodge southwards and follow the railway

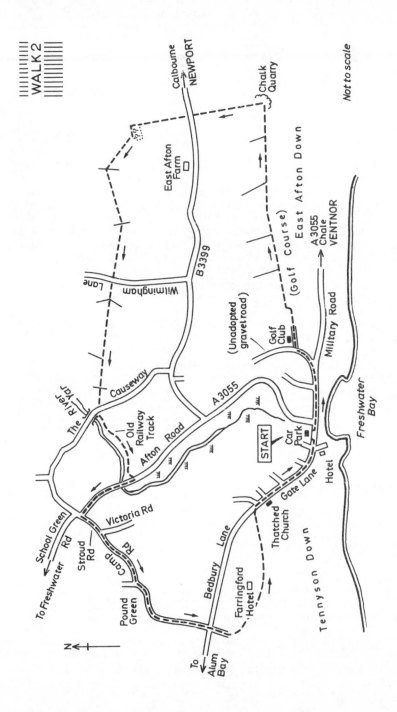

WALK 2

NEWPORT
Calbourne

Chalk Quarry

East Afton Farm

East Afton Down

B3399

Wilmingham Lane

A3055
Chale
VENTNOR

(Golf Course)

(Unadopted gravel road)

Golf Club

Military Road

The River

Causeway

Old Railway Track

Afton Road

A3055

START

Car Park

Hotel

Freshwater Bay

To Freshwater

School Green Rd

Stroud Rd

Camp Rd

Victoria Rd

Pound Green

Bedbury Lane

Gate Lane

Thatched Church

Farringford Hotel

Tennyson Down

To Alum Bay

N

Not to scale

line beside the marshes back to Freshwater. The path emerges 450 yards further on in Afton Road. Turn right and at the crossroads turn left into Stroud Road by the garage. Walk up Stroud Road and bear right into Camp Road on the bend 200 yards beyond. Walk past the old thatched cottages at Pound Green until the road joins Bedbury Lane after 200 yards.

Cross the beautiful tree-lined Bedbury Lane and walk up the track to Sheepwash Farm. Just beyond the farm buildings the path forms a junction. Turn left at this point and follow the path along the southern boundary of Farringford Park. The former home of the Poet Laureate Lord Tennyson lies within its beautiful parkland and glimpses of the castellated 'Gothic' house may be had through the trees. After 600 yards the path rejoins Bedbury Lane opposite its junction with Victoria Road. Turn right down Gate Lane and walk past the little thatched church towards the bay which is sometimes called Freshwater Gate. This name derives from the bay being the only gap or gate in the high cliffs along the south-west coast.

Walk on down Gate Lane passing on the right the large villa called Dimbola which was once the home of Julia Margaret Cameron the pioneer Victorian photographer who was a close friend of her neighbour Lord Tennyson. On reaching the bay cross the road and walk in front of the Albion Hotel to admire the view of the bay in both directions. Behind the hotel the chalk stratification is particularly impressive. The power of the Alpine earth movements can be seen here forcing the chalk from a horizontal to a near vertical position in a giant fold. Return to the main road and turn right, crossing the road to reach the car park and starting point.

Walk 3   Yarmouth and the Yar Valley

$4\frac{1}{2}$ miles (7 km)

This walk covers the low-lying countryside to the south of the historic town of Yarmouth and east of the estuary of the River Yar. The total length of this walk is $4\frac{1}{2}$ miles over low-lying ground.

Ample parking can be found in the town square or in the large car park adjoining River Road to the west of the town centre.

Starting in the centre of the town square turn to face the sea with the church behind you. Walk towards the sea and turn left in the narrow Quay Road opposite the Bugle Hotel. This is the old part of the town which has a long history. In medieval times Yarmouth or Evemuth was the Island's chief town. Baldwin de Redvers, Lord of the Island, granted the town its charter in 1135 and the French attacked on two occasions in 1377 and 1535.

Walk down Quay Road and pass the George Hotel and Yarmouth Castle on the right. The castle was built by Henry VIII in 1538 as one of several coastal defences erected following the earlier visits by the French. In 1547 the castle was completed to an advanced design facilitating the latest principles for providing covering fire from the walls. The castle was strengthened prior to the arrival of the Spanish Armada and later Charles I was held there for a short while.

After the Restoration the Island's governor Sir Robert Holmes built a large house in the garden which was later converted to a hotel. Turn left at the end of Quay Road and cross the road by the taxi rank into River Road. Walk along River Road for 250 yards and follow the road round as it bends to the left. The area beneath this road was once deep harbour with the wall beside the cottages to the left marking the edge of the quay. The estuary was subject to gradual silting up as was the case at Newtown and Brading.

On turning the bend in the road turn right into Mill Road and by the garage carry straight on along the footpath towards the fine old mill. Walk past the mill and after 200 yards cross the old railway line and turn into the field. Follow the path across the field and through Mill Copse. Turn right on leaving the copse and walk alongside the hedge to a lane bounded by hedges on both sides. Continue from the lane along the field boundaries until Wilmingham Lane is reached.

Turn right along the road and walk south for $\frac{1}{2}$ mile. Turn right up a track opposite Wilmingham Farm and after 350 yards bear left and head towards the woodlands which border the river. This path leads to the old railway line. Turn right up the old railway track

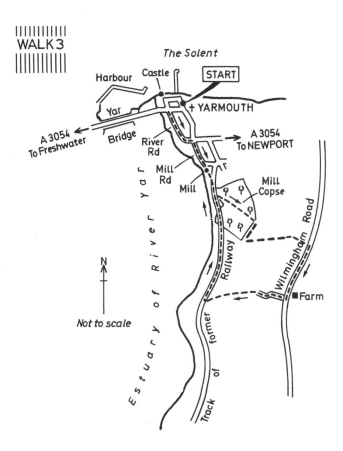

WALK 3

The Solent

Harbour Castle START

Yar

A 3054 To Freshwater   Bridge

River Rd

✝ YARMOUTH

A 3054 To NEWPORT

Mill Rd

Mill

Mill Copse

Estuary of River Yar

N

Not to scale

Railway

Wilmingham Road

Farm

Track of former

which runs between the wood and the river. Follow this path back along the beautiful Yar Valley to the old mill near the starting point of the walk.

23

Walk 4

4 miles (6.5 km)

Compton to Brook

This walk is over downland and cliff tops on the south-west coast in the vicinity of the picturesque village of Brook. It is for the most part easy walking with a short steep section on the inland route from the coast up onto Compton Down.

The starting point is on the A3055 Military Road 1½ miles east of Freshwater Bay. Park in the quarry adjoining the landward side of the road at the point where the road rises steeply alongside the chalk cliffs above Compton Bay.

On leaving the quarry cross the road and turn right, walking up the verge for 200 yards. Enter the field and walk towards the cliff edge to join the coastal footpath. Turn left and continue along the cliff top for 2 miles. The headland by the large car park is Hanover Point and at low tide a fossil raft of pine logs can be seen among the rocks on the foreshore. Continue along the cliff top for another 600 yards and turn inland at Brook Chine where a row of houses lead down to the sea. The old stone building close to the cliff edge is the old lifeboat station from which many rescue attempts once started. This station

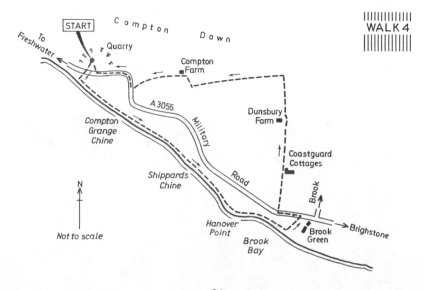

together with those of Atherfield and Chale played an important joint role in saving lives from the one hundred wrecks that occurred along this coast between 1750 and 1850.

On reaching the main road turn left and after 400 yards turn right up the path towards the prominent row of coastguard cottages. Cross the lane in front of the cottages and continue on uphill crossing a second lane after a further 400 yards. Carry straight on uphill to Dunsbury Farm and pass between the farm buildings. Walk up the steep side of the down (which rises some 100 ft in 300 yards) and after 350 yards the path forms a junction with an east-west downland path. Turn left and, with the Freshwater Cliffs ahead, walk towards the coast for $\frac{1}{2}$ mile. After walking gently downhill turn right towards, then head along, the path to Compton Farm which nestles in the valley. On reaching the farm leave the buildings to the right and walk along the lane westwards to the Military Road. Turn right up the road and the car park will be reached after 500 yards.

Walk 5

4½ miles (7 km)

Brook to Mottistone

Many walkers will find this route particularly enjoyable on account of the variety of walking country and the extensive views that the footpaths offer. The walk starts on the coast and after passing north through the village there is a steady uphill gradient to Brook Hill. Turning east the path enters Coombe Plantation which offers delightful glimpses of the sea and coastline before emerging into a sheltered inland chalk valley. The return route is again through woodland until the historic Mottistone Manor is reached and thereafter the walk is over fields and farmland. The total distance of this walk is 4½ miles.

The starting point is at the car park on the A3055 Military Road at Brook Green, which is situated nearly opposite the turning off the main coast road to Brook village.

Turn right out of the National Trust car park at Brook Green and walk along the roadside verge for 200 yards crossing over at the road junction which leads to Brook. Walk inland up this road past Hanover House and through the centre of the village. Continue up the road until Brook Triangle is reached (where the road branches to the right to Brighstone) and carry on up the hill. To the left is Brook House which was built in 1792 for the Bowerman family on the site of a Tudor mansion where Henry VIII once stayed. The house was latterly owned by the First Lord Mottistone's father whose distaste for the advent of the motor car caused him to build, in 1914, a large house in splendid isolation high up on top of Brook Hill to the right. This house was owned more recently by J. B. Priestley who, like his predecessors, must have greatly appreciated the panoramic views that the position offered.

Continue up the road past St Mary's Church (the churchyard of which contains graves to those lost at sea) and the grounds of Brook Hill House which offer superb displays of rhododendrons on the hillside until the driveway to the house is reached at the summit. Turn right up the drive and after 400 yards, and before reaching the house, turn off to the left into the woods. The path is narrow at first but soon widens to a gravelled track. The coast and farmland between the downs and the sea as well as the cliffs towards Freshwater can be seen through the occasional breaks in the woodland to the right. The woodland track is approximately ½ mile in length and bends to the left before emerging onto the downland

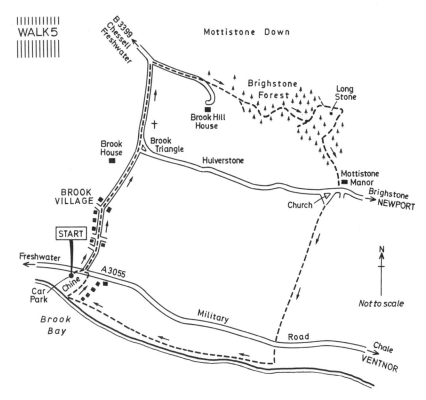

Mottistone Down

B 3399 Chessell Freshwater

Brighstone Forest

Long Stone

Brook Hill House

Brook House

Brook Triangle

Hulverstone

Mottistone Manor

BROOK VILLAGE

Church

Brighstone NEWPORT

START

Freshwater

A 3055

Car Park

Chine

Brook Bay

Military

Road

Chale VENTNOR

N

Not to scale

200 yards later. At this point bear right downhill and after 150 yards opposite an isolated cottage is a clearing with seats at the centre of which is the Long Stone. This megalith of ferruginous sandstone, which is 13 ft high, is believed to be the only visible remains of a long barrow and was probably constructed about 2500 BC.

From the Long Stone cross the clearing downhill and enter the dark path through the woodlands. Walk downhill for 400 yards then bend to the left to join the B3399 at Mottistone village 250 yards later. Mottistone is much photographed and is well worthy of this attention. Mottistone Manor on the north side of the road is a charming L-shaped Elizabethan building with mellowed stone walls and lawned gardens to the front. Two hundred years ago the manor was engulfed by a landslide from the wooded cliffs to the rear and it was buried until 1926 when Lord Mottistone restored it. The church is situated opposite the manor and although extensively restored much of the medieval architecture has been retained.

Cross the main road from the manor and follow the lane to the right-hand side of the green downhill towards the sea. The path is almost straight for ½ mile and eventually joins the Military Road.

27

Cross the road and walk over the field on the seaward side to join the coastal path at the cliff edge. The cliffs in this area are of clay and sandstone and suffer from considerable coastal erosion by the sea during south-westerly gales. Due to undermining it is therefore inadvisable to walk or stand close to the cliff edge.

Turn right along the coastal path and continue for 2 miles. On reaching the houses that form a line between the road and the cliff edge turn right inland to join the road. The starting point of the walk is 250 yards to the left.

Walk 6   Calbourne and Westover

4½ miles (7 km)

The high downs to the west of Newport are covered by pine forests over a considerable area and that part of the north-facing downland between Brook and Calbourne is similarly clothed. This walk starts at Westover Down and follows the edge of the forest before turning north through it down to the village of Calbourne. The return route brings one around the picturesque parkland surrounding Westover House.

The starting point is the car park at the highest point on the road from Calbourne to Brighstone. To reach it turn off the B3401 Newport to Freshwater Road at Calbourne Crossroads and proceed south for 1½ miles.

On leaving the car park walk up the track along the top of the down away from the road. There is a well-worn track which follows the forest edge all the way to Brook. After just over ½ mile turn right through a gate and walk downhill through the wide firebreak in the trees. The view north at this point is across the flat country around the villages of Newbridge, Shalfleet and the arms of the Newtown river and nature reserve can be seen in the distance.

Walk down through the forest for 350 yards crossing an east-west track and on reaching a second track 100 yards later bear left in a wide circle down to the fields at the edge of the forest. Follow the farm track due north to the buildings of Westover Farm. On entering the farmyard turn left down the drive until the road is reached. Turn right along the road past a thatched lodge and up the hill. At the top of the hill one can see Calbourne Water Mill in its beautiful grounds to the left. The mill houses a museum of old agricultural equipment and the stream and riverside walks are maintained to a very high standard. Walk on along the road for another 400 yards and turn right up the farm entrance. Continue for 450 yards across the field beside the Calbourne recreation ground and join the old school lane which leads to the centre of the village.

Calbourne is a most attractive and much photographed village. It comprises thatched and tiled cottages of a most attractive ferruginous stone and although much visited it has not been spoilt by commercialization. Turn left out of the lane and a house on the road edge bears a plaque in memory of William Long, author of *The Isle of Wight Dialect Dictionary*.

To continue the route turn back through the village past the green

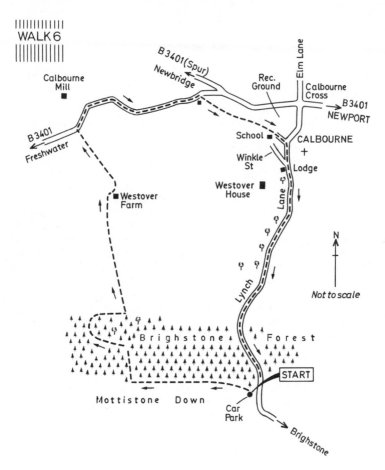

Calbourne
Mill ■

B3401 (Spur)

Newbridge

Elm Lane

Rec.
Ground

Calbourne
Cross

B3401
NEWPORT

B3401
Freshwater

School ■

CALBOURNE
+

Winkle
St

Lodge

Westover ■
House

Lynch Lane

Westover
Farm

N

Not to scale

Brighstone

Forest

START

Mottistone   Down

Car
Park

Brighstone

towards the pond by the Lodge of Westover House. The old church
on the left is of Norman origin but was substantially altered after a
fire in 1683. On reaching the Lodge turn right down the lane to see
'Winkle Street'—a pleasing row of cottages in a sunny position
overlooking a babbling stream. Return to the lodge and turn right
up Lynch Lane. On the right is the imposing Westover House which
was built in the nineteenth century in the classical style. Earlier this
century it was purchased by Octavius Barrett the youngest brother
of Elizabeth Barrett Browning and the house was occupied by his
descendants until recently. Continue along the road and uphill on
the return route. First one passes under the magnificent overhanging
beeches that border the Westover Estate and after ½ mile the road
passes through the Westover forest plantation. On reaching the top
of the hill turn right into the car park where the walk started.

Walk 7   Shalfleet to Newbridge

7 miles (11 km)

The belt of land between the Newtown Estuary to the north and the central chalk downs to the south comprises rich farmlands with oakwoods growing on the heavy clay soils. To the west limestone outcrops on the surface and the stone was quarried some years ago. From Shalfleet a succession of paths lead up the stream known as the Caul Bourn (hence the village of Calbourne) to Newbridge and then west and north to Wellow. The walking is easy and covers a total distance of 7 miles.

The walk starts in Shalfleet village on the A3054 Newport to Yarmouth road where parking is available in the roadside layby outside the church.

From the church turn right along the main road. Turn right again almost immediately into the lane which borders the churchyard. The church itself is very distinctive with its huge, squat Norman tower. The walls of the tower are 5 ft thick and provided safety for residents of the area when foraging French invaders attacked Newtown in the Middle Ages. The tower was once surmounted by a cupola and later a steeple but these were later demolished.

Walk along the lane for 100 yards and where it bends to the right carry on straight ahead along the path which follows the west bank of the Caul Bourn southwards towards the pine-clad downlands of Chessell. Continue on this path for a little under a mile and then cross the old Newport to Freshwater railway line. Directly opposite there is a path which becomes a farm lane a short distance ahead. Keep the farm buildings to the left and follow the lane downhill and over the bridge past the delightful working mill with its pond and race.

Walk on along the lane with the stream below and to the right. At the point where the lane meets the road turn right and at the next road junction continue straight ahead. A short distance ahead on the right is a thatched cottage called Norman's—take the path into the field on the bend in the road at this point. After 100 yards turn right and then right again. On reaching a rough track turn left past Eades Farm and 250 yards later to join Dodpits Lane.

Turn right along Dodpits Lane and walk downhill past Dodpits House (on the right) to the junction with the B3401 spur Thorley to Newbridge road. Cross the road and enter the field directly opposite the junction passing over the old railway line again after 500 yards.

31

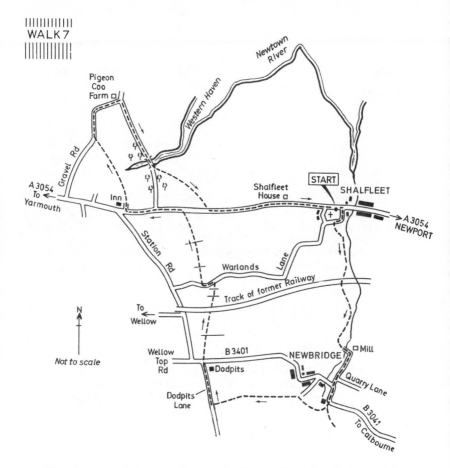

Continue straight ahead towards Lower Dodpits Farm and join
Warlands Lane.

Turn left up the lane and right into the fields by a gentle left-hand
bend in the lane after 200 yards. Cross the fields and pass a small
coppice on the left to join the A3054 Newport to Yarmouth road.
Turn left along the main road and walk past the Horse and Groom
public house to nearly the top of the hill beyond. Just before the
summit turn right along the gravel road which leads past an isolated
row of houses and through open woodland.

After 200 yards bear right to Pigeon Coo Farm and leave the farm
buildings on the left. Beyond the farm the path to the left leads to the
Western Haven of Newtown Marsh which is celebrated for its
birdlife. Turn right here through the woods and follow the main
path due south over a bridge over an arm of the creek towards the

main road again. Beyond the bridge the path forks and the left-hand track should be followed.

Turn left along the A3054 past Shalfleet House and Shalfleet Manor back to the centre of the village. For an extension of this walk which offers a further view of Newtown Creek walk down the hill and turn left by the New Inn which leads to the water's edge.

Walk 8   Newtown Village and Marshes

4 miles (6.5 km)

This walk covers level ground, oakwoods and the salterns in the vicinity of Newtown village within the Newtown Nature Reserve. This historic village lies on the north-west coast of the Island between Porchfield and Shalfleet. Newtown can be reached by turning north off the A3054 Newport to Yarmouth Road by the filling station a few yards on the Newport side of Shalfleet village. When approaching from the south turn left after passing Newtown Old Town Hall and continue past the church to the end of the road. The walk is 4 miles long and will be of particular interest to ornithologists for the wide variety of waders, ducks and other species that have been recorded there.

The walk starts at the car park at the western end of the village.

From the end of the road walk through the gate and along the narrow path for 100 yards. Pass through a second gate and walk along the edge of the field beside the hedge towards the estuary. At the far side of the field pass through the gate and take the footbridge out onto the old sea wall. The wall and path curve around the marsh to the north-east but, although there was once a complete circular path, unrepaired breaches of the sea wall many years ago mean returning via the same route.

Having walked as far as desired along the sea wall return over the long footbridge and instead of returning through the gate ahead turn left along the path around the edge of the marsh. After 150 yards turn right up the track that joins Newtown village road by Marsh Farm. On reaching the road turn left through the gate into the field. This long narrow field was once one of the village streets in more prosperous times.

Newtown is the oldest of the boroughs of the Isle of Wight and the village was once far greater than the remains indicate. The Newtown Estuary once formed a large deep-water harbour where the greatest of English warships used to berth. However the gradual silting up of the estuary caused a decline in its status as a major south-coast port. The village was formerly named Franchville and a plaque to this effect is situated over the entrance of the long-closed public house the Franchville Arms. It was the French who sacked the town in 1377 but the port survived this and still accommodated part of the Armada Fleet in Queen Elizabeth I's reign.

In the eighteenth and nineteenth centuries the harbour silted up

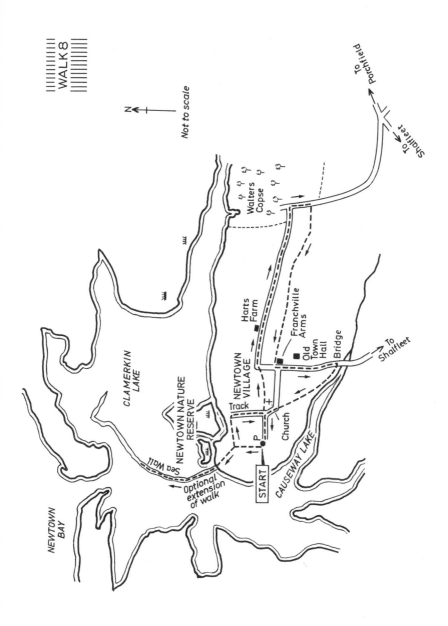

WALK 8

N

Not to scale

NEWTOWN BAY

CLAMERKIN LAKE

Sea Wall

NEWTOWN NATURE RESERVE

Optional extension of walk

START

P

Track

NEWTOWN VILLAGE

Church

CAUSEWAY LAKE

Harts Farm

Walters Copse

Franchville Arms

Old Town Hall

Bridge

To Shalfleet

To Shalfleet

To Porchfield

causing residents to change their business to oyster fishing and obtaining salt. Newtown struggled on and continued to send two members to Parliament until 1832. There are few relics of Newtown's important past, the town hall being the only prominent building. This was erected in 1699 and was carefully restored some years ago by a group of benefactors known as The Ferguson Gang who handed it over completed to the National Trust.

Walk through the field beside the hedge and leave through the gate at the far end. Cross the verge and walk straight down the road in front leaving the marsh to the left. Walk along the quiet road past Harts Farm and after 400 yards follow the road round the sharp turn to the right. This length of road is bordered by oakwoods and is very lightly trafficked. As a result many species of woodland birds may be seen, jays being particularly abundant. After 150 yards turn right into the field and walk back alongside the hedge towards the village. After 600 yards the path emerges beside the Franchville Arms. To the left is the old town hall which is open to the public. Walk down the hill past the town hall and on reaching the small stone bridge which arches over an arm of the estuary turn right following the sign to the village. The return path follows the edge of the marsh and then swings inland emerging 200 yards later on in the centre of the village by the church. Turn left around the corner to reach the car park.

Walk 9   Shorwell to Brighstone Down

8 miles (13 km)

The many footpaths over the downs behind Shorwell and Brighstone provide delightful walks with good coastal and inland views. In addition the wild flowers of the chalk and several species of woodland and downland bird will be seen.

This walk starts at the Footpath Centre adjoining the B3323 Newport to Shorwell road immediately north of Shorwell village. Parking is available in the quarry on the left-hand side of Shorwell Shute near the point where a fine, recently constructed, rustic footbridge spans the road. The path leads from here in a circle northwards and westwards before descending into Shorwell village. The route is steady, vigorous walking covering a total of nearly 8 miles.

Cross the road from the car park to the opposite side and enter The Dell of trees above Northcourt House. Take the footpath marked with a yellow arrow and signposted for Chillerton. This path leads immediately over the road by means of the footbridge. Walk through the wood for 150 yards then turn right into a field. Follow the track along the lower boundary and on entering the next field turn gently leftward (north-eastwards) climbing slightly. Below on the right a track can be seen running along the bottom of the valley to Newbarn Farm.

After about ½ mile a gate is reached and a track runs from here ahead and to the right up towards the television mast at Chillerton Down. From this gate a path runs up to this track joined a little way by the path from Newbarn Farm below. Follow this track and on reaching the concrete access lane to the TV station turn left down to the Shorwell–Newport road.

Turn right down the road and after ½ mile Rowborough Farm will be reached. Turn left up the lane just beyond the farm buildings and after just over ½ mile, where the lane wiggles to the left and enters a field, leave it and continue along the footpath which now becomes a broad grassy track. Follow on through the woodland on Rowborough Down and then cross the bottom of a second field and through more woodland. At this point the path turns southwards and comes to a junction. Carry straight ahead over this cross track and at the second such junction follow the finger-post to Brighstone Down along the Tennyson Trail.

Leave the wood by means of the gate and walk out onto the open

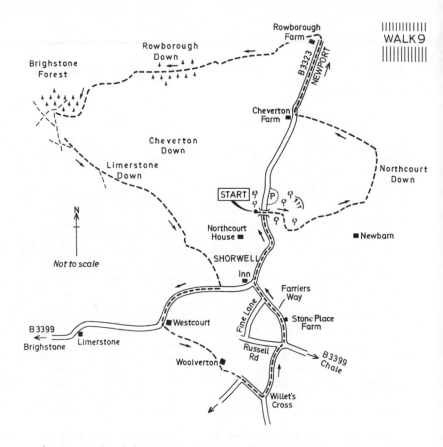

downs turning left along the Worsley Trail back towards Shorwell.

The return route to Shorwell follows a track which climbs to the summit of Limerstone Down. Near the top a small stone pillar surmounted by a metal disc (the Quinn-Smith Monument) indicates the direction and distances of a number of more or less remote towns or localities such as Ryde, Newport, London, John O'Groats and Cherbourg.

A mile beyond this point turn right off the crest of the down and walk down the side of the hill to Shorwell village. The first 300 yards is virtually straight down the hillside and then the path turns left to border the Northcourt Estate to emerge on the B3399 just west of Shorwell village.

The downland section of this walk ends at this point and a fine selection of chalk-hill flowers are to be seen. These include eyebright, red bartsia, houndstongue, autumn gentian, vervain and a white variant of the musk mallow.

Turn right along the road and follow the bend round to the left. On the corner will be seen the fine old manor of Westcourt, a rambling building which was built in 1579. Turn left down the lane immediately beyond Westcourt and walk downhill crossing the stream in the valley. Walk up the other side through a wood and emerge at the rear of the recently restored Woolverton Manor. This manor of beautiful local stone was built by John Dingley in about 1630. Walk up the drive between the manor and some old farm buildings to emerge on a minor road. Walk straight ahead up the road and turn left at the road junction 250 yards ahead. Walk down the road and into Shorwell village along Farriers Way. Pass the old Stone Place Farm on the right and continue until the junction of the B3399 by Shorwell church.

The church of St Peter is for the most part over 500 years old. In 1610 the spire was rebuilt and an extension was added to the south aisle to house the Parish Gun. Walk on uphill past some very pleasant 'Shorwell Stone' and thatched seventeenth-century cottages and past the entrance to Northcourt House. The large rambling manor-house can be seen among the trees on the left. This is the largest Jacobean manor on the Island and was built by Sir John Leigh in 1615. A short distance up the hill will be seen the footbridge that crosses the road by the Footpath Centre.

Walk 10   Chale to Blackgang

6½ miles (10.5 km)

This walk covers the cliff tops and high downland behind Blackgang and Chale on the south-west coast of the Island. It commences at Whale Chine and follows the coastline to Blackgang before rising to the summit of St Catherine's Down on which an historic old lighthouse is situated. The return route takes the walker down the western slopes and across the open country by Chale Green until the coast is reached again at the Military Road.

The first part of the walk is on gently rising ground before a steeper section of 1 mile which leads to the summit of the down. The remainder is a level or gently sloping walk back to the car park.

Whale Chine car park lies on the A3055 Military Road 1 mile west of Chale.

From the car park walk back towards Chale along the roadside verge for 300 yards and turn right across the field to the cliff edge. Turn left and follow the coastal path for 600 yards. Chale Bay (below to the right) is notorious for the number of wrecks that have occurred there; over one hundred ships sank in the vicinity between 1750 and 1850. Bear left inland and return to the Military Road 200 yards west of Chale church. Turn right and walk along the verge past the church and 30 yards further on turn right into the lane called Chale Terrace. Chale church once lay in the centre of Chale parish. A short walk to the end of this road will show how much of the cliff edge has fallen away. Several houses of 'The Terrace' have since been lost as a result.

After 100 yards bear left off the lane and continue up the hill to rejoin the A3055 by the Blackgang road turnoff. A short diversion at this point leads one to the popular Blackgang Chine with its spectacular scenery, museum and many other attractions. Cross the main road and walk up Blythe Shute following the left-hand verge. After ¼ mile take the steps up the bank (opposite the entrance to the viewpoint car park) and continue straight across the field and over the three stiles to the old lighthouse on the top of St Catherine's Down. The summit here is at a height of 718 ft above sea level (only slightly lower than St Boniface Down at Ventnor, 787 ft, the Island's highest point).

The old lighthouse was erected by Walter De Godeton in 1314 as penance for stealing a cargo of holy wine from a ship in Chale Bay. A mile to the north of the lighthouse can be seen the tall pillar known

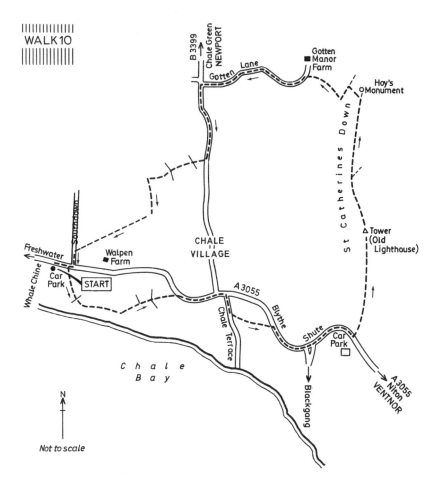

B 3399

Chale Green
NEWPORT

Gotten
Manor
Farm

Gotten   Lane

Hoy's
○ Monument

St Catherines Down

△ Tower
(Old
Lighthouse)

CHALE
VILLAGE

Freshwater

Whale Chine

Car
Park

Walpen
Farm

START

A 3055

Chale Terrace

Blythe

Shute

Car
Park

A 3055
Niton
VENTNOR

C h a l e
B a y

Blackgang

N

Not to scale

as Hoy's Monument. Continue due north for 400 yards and join the footpath which leads straight to Hoy. Spectacular views of the whole of the 'back of the Wight' between Chale and the Needles can be seen to the left whilst the gentle rolling inland farming landscape is well portrayed in the valley to the right. After inspecting the monument (which was erected by Michael Hoy in memory of a visit by Alexander, Emperor of Russia) bear left from the National Trust sign down the track towards Chale Green. After walking 200 yards downhill turn sharp left and continue for 200 yards. At this point turn right down the track until it joins the farm lane. Turn left up the lane and over the hill before descending to the B3399 Chale to Chale Green road. Turn left and walk along the roadside for ¼ mile then turn right through the gate and across the fields until a farm

41

track is reached. Continue along the track past Walpen Farm and Tuttons Hill Cottage to emerge in Southdown Lane. Turn left and after 200 yards join the Military Road. Whale Chine car park lies 400 yards further on to the right.

Walk 11   Blackgang to Niton

5 miles (8 km)

This walk covers some of the most spectacular and widely contrasting scenery to be found on the Island. It commences at Blackgang, a small coastal village on the A3055 and continues eastwards to the old smuggling village of Niton via the coastal path along the top of Gore Cliff. From Niton the path leads to the sea at Puckaster Cove and then the return route follows the old disused Niton–Blackgang road, a part of which was swept away by the great landslide of 1927.

The stretch of country along the south coast of the Isle of Wight is known as The Undercliff and comprises a ½-mile wide shelf of fallen ground which affords a luxuriant growth of vegetation on account of the mild and very sunny climate.

Blackgang Viewpoint can be reached by driving to either Chale or Niton and joining the A3055. The car park is situated ½ mile between the two villages immediately adjacent to the main road near the top of St Catherine's Down.

From the far end of the car park walk up the steps and along the path to the cliff edge. Before turning left by the seat pause to admire 'the back of the Wight'—the name given to the 12-mile length of coastline between Chale and Freshwater. There is a long history of wrecks and smuggling in the area and Blackgang was named after one infamous band of men. Follow the cliff edge eastwards to Niton village. On your left at the top of St Catherine's Down is the old lighthouse which was erected by Walter De Godeton as penance for stealing a cargo of holy wine. Continue past the radio station and downhill to the village.

On reaching the main road cross over and walk up the lane opposite. Turn right after 80 yards and then bear right again 30 yards further on. The path emerges from a tunnel of trees opposite St Catherine's Terrace on the A3055. Turn left along the main road and continue for 450 yards. As the road enters the woods cross over by the Niton village sign. Here there is a path which leads to Puckaster Cove. Continue down through the woodland and turn right at the cliff edge. After 500 yards bear right uphill past Puckaster Cottage until you reach the road.

Turn left and continue for 400 yards leaving the historic Buddle Inn on your right. (Buddle means 'a place where tin ore is washed' and bartering took place in Puckaster Cove 2,000 years ago as the Island lay on the old tin route between Cornwall and Marseilles.)

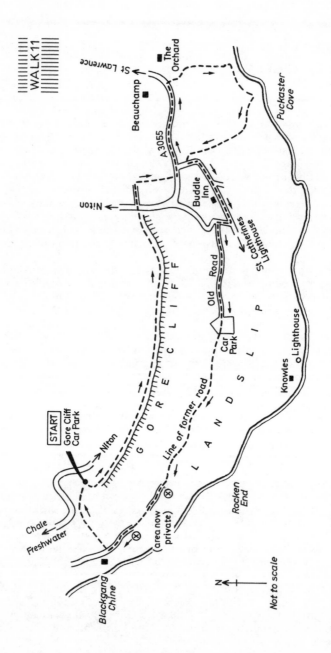

WALK 11

The Orchard

St Lawrence

Beauchamp

Puckaster Cove

A3055

Niton

Buddle Inn

St Catherines Lighthouse

G O R E   C L I F F

Old   Road

L A N D S L I P

START
Gore Cliff
Car Park

Niton

Car Park

Line of former road

Knowles

Lighthouse

Chale

Freshwater

(area now private)

Rocken End

Blackgang Chine

N

Not to scale

About 100 yards past the inn follow the road round to the right uphill and then turn left after 80 yards.

You are now walking along the old coast road a $\frac{1}{4}$-mile section of which is missing following the landslide over fifty years ago. The high greensand and chert cliffs to the right are a striking feature and the crevices are inhabited by kestrels whilst the fallen rocks are very fossiliferous.

On reaching the car park at the end of the road bear right through the gap in the fence by the National Trust sign and follow the track down, then right and up over the bluff. On reaching the top there is a fine view of the whole mass of the Undercliff with the new lighthouse (the brightest in Europe) below. Follow the path down the seaward side of the bluff and continue across the landslip to the Blackgang side. Here the old road is rejoined for a short distance before crossing a second path to the terminus of Blackgang Old Road. The section of path between the two points shown on the map was public highway but has been formally abandoned because of land movement. However, the owner is quite agreeable to the continued use of this walk. Walk up the road to the entrance to Blackgang Chine and turn right up the hill by means of the footpath opposite. Halfway up the hill bear right up the steep path which leads to the starting point.

Walk 12

6 miles (9.5 km)

Niton to St Lawrence

This walk commences in the centre of Niton village and continues southwards and then eastwards along the top of the rugged Undercliff to St Lawrence. Here the route leads to the coast and back to Niton via the coastal path. The walk is for the most part gentle with a gradual descent and ascent at either end.

The starting point is the public car park at the rear of the youth club at Niton.

Emerge from the car park and turn left, crossing the road by the pub in the centre of the village. Turn right on reaching the pavement on the opposite side of the road and walk up the hill for 100 yards. Turn left down the lane leading to Niton School and walk past the school and along the narrow footpath at the end of the lane.

Niton was renowned at the turn of the century as a smugglers' village and there are many stories of how the residents of the day hid their contraband from the customs men. It is uncertain whether some of the residents indulged in wrecking by placing decoy lights in Chale Bay. However, this was overcome by the construction of a new lighthouse at St Catherine's Point in 1838.

The footpath from the school bends sharply to the left and then to the right. After 200 yards bear left and the cliff-top path will be reached shortly. Turn left and the walk continues along the cliff edge for 1¼ miles. The sheltered belt of ground below to the right is known as the Undercliff and is covered with a rich growth of vegetation well suited to the mild sunny climate. Rich families built large villas along the coast and spent summer holidays here for recreation and health reasons. Immediately below the junction of the Niton path and the cliff path is The Orchard. This house was bought, in 1817, by Sir Willoughby Gordon, Baronet, who was ADC to the Duke of Wellington in the Peninsular War.

Continue along the cliff top for a further mile. At St Lawrence Shute the path drops down to road level. Turn right down the hill and cross the bridge over the former railway line. Turn sharp left at the road junction by the old station into Seven Sisters Road. After 100 yards turn right down the path by St Lawrence Old Church. This church was the smallest in England until the nave was extended and it is well worth inspecting. Some of the gravestones also offer interesting inscriptions. Follow the path downhill for 100 yards until it joins the main A3055 road, Undercliff Drive. Turn left

WALK 12

and after 50 yards turn right into Woolverton Road. Walk down the hill and bear to the left down a gravel track towards the sea after 150 yards. To the right is Woolverton Manor a most attractive old stone house with a ruined chapel in the grounds. At the end of the track climb over the stile and walk across the field to the hill on the cliff edge known as Sugarloaf. A short climb to the summit gives a picturesque view of the coastline of sandstone and chalk cliffs. Looking inland the face of the Undercliff stretches to the west and east with its thick covering of evergreen oak and other rich vegetation.

From the base of the hill continue westwards along the coastal path. Continue west leaving Old Park Hotel on your right and at the next headland, known as Binnel Point, follow the footpath to the right for 350 yards. On reaching the main Undercliff Drive turn left along this beautiful tree-shrouded road and at the Niton village sign turn left down the steep track leading to the sea. On reaching the cliff top turn right and follow the curve of Puckaster Cove westwards. After 200 yards at the headland dividing this bay from Reeth Bay to the west turn right inland. In 1810 an hotel called 'The Victoria Lodging House' was actually built on the beach at Reeth Bay. It was a large and very fashionable building of forty bedrooms and was popular for a number of years before being undermined by the sea.

Walk uphill and inland from the cliff top for $\frac{1}{2}$ mile and turn right into the minor road at the top. After 50 yards cross the main road and enter the path on the opposite side. Continue up through this 'tunnel' through the trees and after emerging into the field walk on for 100 yards. Turn left on reaching the lane and then right at the junction with the main road. Continue on this footpath up the hill and then down into Niton village to the car park.

Walk 13

3½ miles (5.5 km)

Gatcombe to Blackwater

This walk covers the scenery that is typical of the inland Wight. This hill and vale landscape surrounds the upper reaches of the River Medina and comprises woodlands and rich farmlands, on which several fine country houses are situated. The route is over easy walking ground and covers a total distance of 6 miles.

The walk starts at Gatcombe church where there is a parking area adjacent to the roadside. The church can be reached by taking the Newport–Chillerton road and turning off to the right at the signpost to Gatcombe after 3½ miles.

Park by the entrance to the churchyard and walk up the track through the woods away from the road. Gatcombe is perhaps the most secluded of inland villages set below the downs and the name means 'gateway to the valley'. The church is thirteenth century with a Perpendicular style tower that was restored by Sir Charles Seely, an island benefactor, in 1922.

Walk on up the hill and down the opposite side to join the farm lane by a group of cottages. On the left is the Gatcombe Estate with a fine Georgian manor-house built by Sir Edward Worsley in 1710. Where the lane diverges to the left carry straight on and join the Chillerton road by the ford 300 yards further on. Turn left along the road and then right up the hill opposite Sheat Manor (a fine Jacobean house), after 350 yards. From the top of the hill continue along the road to Loverstone Farm (where there is a steel-work depot) and turn left down across the fields just past the farmhouse. Proceed to the bottom of the field and cross the River Medina headwaters over the footbridge. Cross two fields on the way up the far hillside and join the lane leading to Sibdown Farm. Do not take the farm lane but walk on for 10 yards then turn left along the path which joins the A3020 Newport to Shanklin road at Rookley village. Turn left and walk along the wide verge and cross the road opposite the village hall. The footpath leading from the opposite side of the road takes the walker over an open down to join Birchmore Farm Lane beside an isolated brick cottage.

Turn left along the lane over two cattle grids and bear right past Birchmore Farm. Continue along the lane for 800 yards to join the A3020 by a pair of thatched cottages.

Turn right along the main road and left down the lane after 100 yards. Walk down the lane and turn left through the gate into the

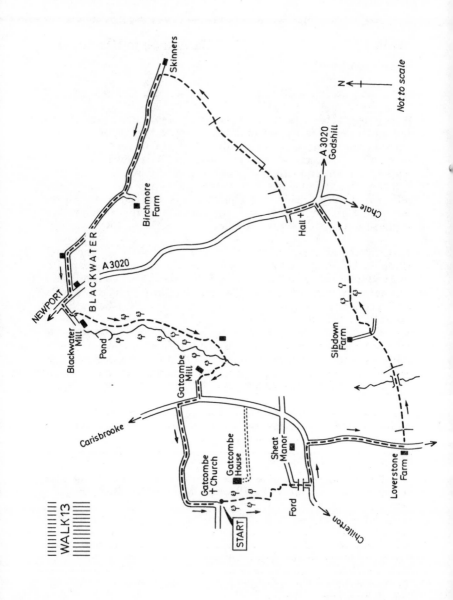

WALK 13

Skinners

Birchmore Farm

BLACKWATER

NEWPORT

A 3020

Blackwater Mill

Pond

Gatcombe Mill

Carisbrooke

Gatcombe
+ Church

Gatcombe
House

START

Ford

Sheat
Manor

Chillerton

Hall +

A 3020
Godshill

Chale

Sibdown
Farm

Loverstone
Farm

N

Not to scale

field just before the entrance to Blackwater Millhouse. Bear right and follow the path alongside the fence and adjacent mill pond. Continue beside the River Medina for a further $\frac{1}{2}$ mile until Champion Farm is reached. Bear to the right of the farm and then right down through the woods to the river—the path following a zig-zag course near the bottom. Cross the stream and turn right to Gatcombe Mill a distance of 100 yards. At the house turn left up the lane to meet the Newport–Chillerton road.

Turn right and after 250 yards turn left up the quiet road to Gatcombe village. Pass the lake in the grounds of Gatcombe House to the left and follow the winding road for 300 yards until the church and starting point of the walk is rejoined.

Walk 14   Newport to Gatcombe
8 miles (13 km)

This walk starts in the heart of the Island's capital within the conservation area and leads out of the town southwards through the villages of Blackwater and Gatcombe before returning to Newport via Carisbrooke. The walk will be of particular interest to those who like architecture as many distinguished buildings are passed on the route.

Newport has been described by various authors over the centuries. It was described by Sir John Oglander of Nunwell as 'a poor sort of place' in the sixteenth century. However after extensive rebuilding in the Georgian period the town was considerably improved. George Brannon in his *Picture of the Isle of Wight* described the town as follows: 'Newport is allowed by most travellers to be as clean and pretty a country town as any in the Kingdom. The houses are of a modern and respectable construction, the streets regular and well-paved, with sufficient descent to be always clean.'

The walk is over easy ground and covers 8 miles. The starting point is in the centre of Newport in St Thomas' Square and parking can be found nearby in several of the town's car parks.

Walk to the centre of St Thomas' Square and pause by the war memorial. The square is dominated by the church, built as late as 1854, which stands in its piazza. Relics from a much earlier building including a fine Jacobean panelled pulpit and font are the best features of the building. In the north aisle there is a marble tomb in memory of Princess Elizabeth, the daughter of Charles I who died in Carisbrooke Castle. Opposite the eastern end of the church is God's Providence House (now a tea-room), so named because the occupants were spared by the Plague.

Turn to face south, cross the road and walk down a wide path next to a large new store. It is worth noticing the finely restored fascia of the Mechanics Institute on the right. Emerge onto the busy South Street opposite the bus station and walk up the road opposite entering Litten Park just by the entrance to a small car park by the crossroads. Bear left across the park and after 200 yards emerge on the junction of Church Litten and Medina Avenue. Cross the road and turn left along Medina Avenue. Follow the road round the corner to the right and walk along Medina Avenue until it meets Shide Road at the far end.

The large house, Shide Villa, on this junction was once the home

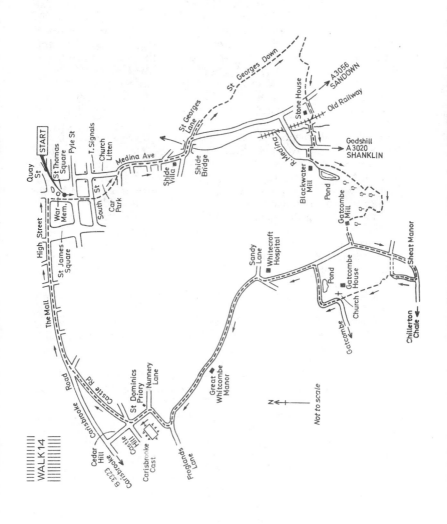

WALK 14

START

Quay St
St Thomas Square
Pyle St
T. Signals
Church Litten
Medina Ave

War. Mem.
High Street
South St
Car Park

St James Square

The Mall

St Dominics Priory
Nunnery Lane

Carisbrooke Road
Castle Rd
Cedar Hill
B 3323
Carisbrooke Castle
Castle Hill

Froglands Lane

Great Whitcombe Manor

Shide Villa
Shide Bridge

St Georges Lane
St Georges Down

Stone House
Old Railway
A3056 SANDOWN

R. Medina
Godshill
A 3020 SHANKLIN

Blackwater Mill
Pond

Gatcombe Mill
Sheat Manor

Sandy Lane
Whitecroft Hospital
Pond
Gatcombe House
Gatcombe Church

Chillerton
Chale

N

Not to scale

of Professor 'Earthquake' Milne, a pioneer geologist who, for twenty years, was employed by the Japanese Government. He established the seismic survey of Japan which embraced 968 stations and was a diligent author and researcher. He established an observatory at Shide Villa and worked there until his death in 1913.

Turn left along Shide Road and cross the bridge over the River Medina. Cross the road on the bend and walk up St George's Lane to the right (which runs steeply uphill behind the houses fronting the main road A3020). Continue up to the top of the lane which allows excellent views over the farmland to the west. Keep to the path passing the golf club on the left. The ground in this vicinity has a thick cap of gravel which has been extensively worked for road materials.

Nearly $\frac{1}{2}$ mile beyond the golf club there is a crossroads of paths (Garretts to the left and Standen House below to the right). Continue straight on for another $\frac{1}{2}$ mile and at this second crossing of paths turn back sharp right along the track which leads downhill to Blackwater. Pass over some old gravel workings and then descend straight down the hillside joining the A3056 by a roadside depot.

Turn left along the main road and after 200 yards cross over and walk down the lane past Stone House. Turn right at the bottom of the lane and after 150 yards enter the field by the gate and cross over to the far side following the hedgerow. Leave the field at the bottom and pass through some trees before crossing a footbridge. The A3020 Newport to Shanklin road is 200 yards ahead.

Turn right along the main road and after 50 yards cross over and walk down the lane to the recently modernized Blackwater Mill. Turn left into the field just before the mill and follow the fence along the edge of the large field which bounds the millpond. Follow the river and woodland edge for nearly a mile until Champion Farm is reached. Bear to the right of the farm and follow a winding track eventually crossing the river just before reaching Gatcombe Mill.

Walk up the lane from the Mill until it reaches the Carisbrooke to Chillerton Road. Turn left along the road passing the fine classical Gatcombe House on the right. This house was built by Sir Edward Worsley in 1710 and is somewhat similar to, although smaller than, Appuldurcombe. Continue along the road for $\frac{3}{4}$ mile and follow it round a right-hand bend into Chillerton village. Just past the bend on the right is the seventeenth-century Sheat Manor. This manor was built for the Urry family and is one of a number of small manors, of a most pleasing architectural style, in the area.

Turn right 300 yards beyond the manor and walk up the lane by the stream. Walk up the hill to the top and then descend through the woods to the Gatcombe Road beside Gatcombe church. For an extension of this walk turn left to the hamlet of Gatcombe. Turn right along the road (passing the grounds of Gatcombe House on the right) to emerge on the Chillerton–Carisbrooke road.

Turn left along this pleasant rural road and pass Whitecroft

Hospital on the right. Continue on this road for a further mile passing the delightfully proportioned red-brick mansion, Great Whitcombe Manor, on the left. At the top of the hill Carisbrooke Castle will be seen directly ahead. Turn right along the road passing St Dominic's Priory on the bend on the right-hand side. Walk on downhill to Fiveways junction and bear right down Castle Road to join Carisbrooke Road.

At this junction cross the pedestrian crossing and follow the elevated Mall to the right into Newport. The row of houses along this road is dignified and forms a well-proportioned terrace. At the eastern end join High Street which leads straight to the town centre and starting point of the walk.

Walk 15   Carisbrooke to Bowcombe

3 miles (5 km)

The high downs in the vicinity of Carisbrooke provide a number of excellent walks from which the imposing castle fortifications can be seen. The village of Carisbrooke with its leafy lanes and fords provides a contrast to the downs behind.

This walk starts at the viewpoint car park in Whitcombe Road, Carisbrooke, opposite St Dominic's Priory. It can be reached by taking the Freshwater Road (B3323) from Newport and turning left up Cedar Hill ½ mile to the west of the town. Continue up the hill for ½ mile and the car park lies at the summit on the right-hand side of the road. This route is short, covering only 3 miles but the landscape is varied and all aspects of the castle can be seen from the paths.

Turn right out of the car park (walking away from the priory) and walk along the road edge for 300 yards. At the bend in the road turn right down the narrow Froglands Lane. After 400 yards the lane turns downhill to the right but you carry straight on past Froglands Farm. Walk along the path for a further 700 yards and then turn right to join a grassy track, 400 yards later. Turn right and join the lane by Plaish walking in front of the farmhouse and enter the water meadows to the left of the farm buildings. Follow the course of the Lukely Brook towards Carisbrooke Castle which is on the summit of the hill ahead. Continue across the next field and walk alongside the hedge slightly to the right until Clatterford Shute is reached.

On joining the lane the stream forms a ford over the road surface. Turn right at this point and after 100 yards by the lane junction take the signposted footpath up to the castle at the point where the two lanes meet. After a steady climb of 200 yards this track emerges in the main car park immediately to the west of the castle entrance. Turn left and walk along the edge of the car park pausing to examine the excellent view of the pretty village of Carisbrooke with its old church immediately to the north. Continue for another 300 yards to the castle entrance.

At this point it is worth describing briefly the history and structure of the castle as the walker will have observed every view of it during the course of the journey.

Of the castles on the Island, Carisbrooke is of greatest importance on account of its historical association with Charles I. The castle is built on high ground and is of a rectangular design. The keep occupies the north-east corner of the fortifications whilst the

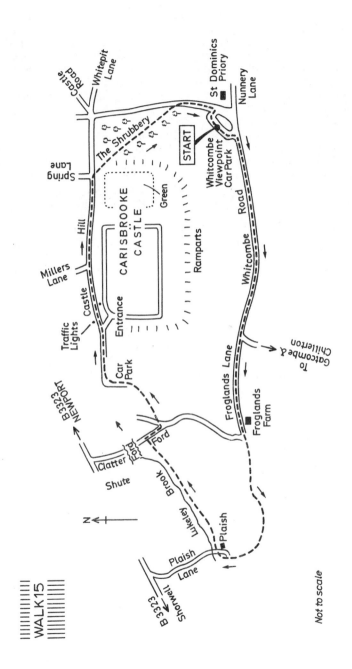

WALK 15

Whitepit Lane

Castle Road

The Shrubbery

St Dominics Priory

Nunnery Lane

START

Whitcombe Viewpoint Car Park

Spring Lane

CARISBROOKE CASTLE

Green

Hill

Ramparts

Millers Lane

Whitcombe Road

Castle

Traffic Lights

Entrance

Car Park

Froglands Lane

To Gatcombe & Chillerton

B3323 NEWPORT

Car Park

Froglands Farm

Ford

Clatter Ford

Shute

Lukeley Brook

Plaish

N

Plaish Lane

B 3323 Shorwell

Not to scale

gatehouse and entrance-way are to the north-west. The whole structure is surrounded by a system of bulwarks with a barbican between the inner and outer walls. Its construction and development took place during Roman, medieval and Elizabethan times with the greater part of the structure being built about 1136. The keep and the curtain walls were probably the earliest medieval constructions, the chapel and domestic buildings having been commenced about 1270, and further additions and improvements were made between 1582 and 1603.

Apart from the imprisonment of King Charles it also played an important role in the twelfth century when Baldwin de Redvers, who sided with Maud against King Stephen, retreated to the Isle of Wight where he was under siege from the King. Today the keep, well-house (with its wheel turned by donkeys) and Governor's House are well preserved and house an interesting museum of the Island's history.

Continue down the hill past the gatehouse taking care to negotiate the corner where a bulwark necessitates the use of traffic lights. Up to the right on the outer wall is the window from which King Charles attempted his escape. However he was unable to pass through the gap and required assistance to free himself. Leaving the castle on the right walk on towards Newport past the point where a road joins from the left and opposite the second junction (Spring Lane) turn right up the track through the mature woodlands alongside the castle grounds. Walk uphill for 300 yards and at the end of the path turn left to rejoin Whitcombe Road. Turn right up the hill to enter Whitcombe viewpoint car park 300 yards later.

Walk 16

8 miles (13 km)

This walk starts on The Parade at West Cowes seafront and offers a route with excellent opportunities for viewing the Solent yachts, coastal-craft and liners that use Cowes Roads. The path follows the north-west coast beyond Gurnard to turn inland near Thorness before returning to Cowes through Northwood and the pleasant residential parts of the town. The route is easy walking with gentle gradients and covers a total distance of 8 miles.

The starting point is on Cowes promenade (known as The Parade) where there is ample free long term parking space available.

Step onto the wide, paved footway adjoining the sea-wall and turn left, walking to the large building which projects out towards the sea. This is the Royal Yacht Squadron and the sea-wall passes around the seaward side of its ramparts. This building was formerly West Cowes Castle and was erected by Henry VIII in 1538 for the purpose of defending the mouth of the River Medina. The stone for its construction came from part of Beaulieu Abbey which was being altered at that time. The castle was used as a prison in the late seventeenth century and was purchased by the Royal Yacht Squadron in 1856.

Sailing was popularized by the Duke of Gloucester after his visit to Cowes in 1811 and he started the club under the leadership of the Earl of Yarborough in 1817. After the Prince Consort became a member the pastime was given a further boost with a markedly beneficial effect on the town of Cowes.

Continue past the Squadron and Princes Green and carry on along the sea-wall for a further mile. On reaching the Woodvale Hotel join the road and carry on up the narrow Shore Road which winds to the cliff top to join Worsley Road. Walk up Worsley Road for 200 yards and then turn right, down Solent View Road. At the bottom of the road carry straight on along Marsh Road and on crossing the bridge at the western end turn right down the cul-de-sac towards the sea. Turn left after 50 yards and walk up along the high cliff tops above Thorness Bay. Carry on along the cliff top until the path descends to an estuary by a large pylon which marks an underwater cable. Turn inland here and walk along the farm lane away from the sea past Whippance Farm until the road is reached $\frac{1}{2}$ mile further on.

Turn left up the road leaving Hillis Farm on the left-hand side.

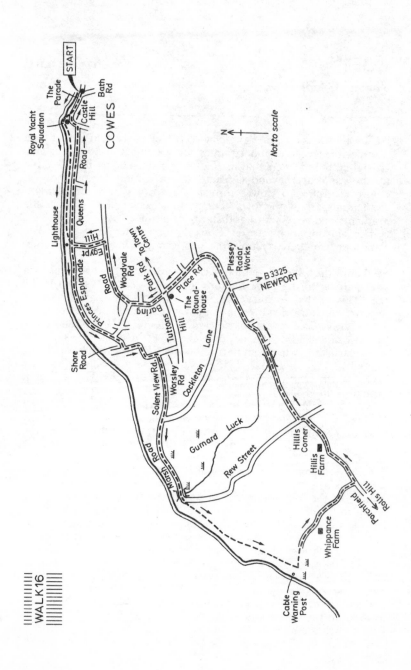

WALK 16

About 400 yards beyond the farm turn left and then right along Pallance Road. The first part of this road is rural but after ¼ mile the stream known as Gurnard Luck is crossed and the next ¾ mile is built up. At the top of Pallance Road turn left past the Plessey Radar works and continue along Place Road until the road joins Park Road by the circular lodge known as The Roundhouse. Turn left and then right immediately along the peaceful residential Baring Road which allows views through the trees to the Solent.

Follow the curve of Baring Road for 600 yards and turn left down Egypt Hill to the Princes Esplanade. At the bottom of the hill turn right and walk along Queens Road until it joins Castle Hill immediately behind the Royal Yacht Squadron. Turn left down Castle Hill to emerge at The Parade, the starting point of the walk.

Walk 17

8 miles (13 km)

Newport to Whippingham

There are few footpaths across the countryside north of Newport and to the south of Cowes, but an extremely popular walk follows the east bank of the River Medina northwards from Newport Old Quay to Whippingham church. The route is over level ground for the most part with some gentle inclines at the halfway point. The circular route returns to Newport through farmland via Whippingham and Staplers making a total length of 8 miles.

The starting point is the large public car park beside Coppins Roundabout at the point where the A3054 Ryde–Newport and A3020 Cowes–Newport roads meet to the east of the town centre.

Leave the car park by the roundabout entrance and walk along the pavement crossing to the opposite side by a grassed area with seats. Walk up the hill for 50 yards and bear left into A3054 Fairlee Road. Continue along the footpath for 200 yards and turn left into Hillside opposite a row of advertising hoardings. At the bottom of Hillside Road enter the quay and walk straight ahead towards the River Medina. To the left is the old quay at which vessels unloaded a wide range of bulk goods and general merchandise for centuries. The old warehouses and other fine listed buildings are in process of being restored.

Turn right along the quay past the warehouses and follow the riverside path northwards for 2 miles. The walk takes one past Seaclose Park on the right and then Fairlee Villa before reaching the causeway at Wight Marina. On emerging from the copse keep to the left of the first lake and walk past the two old vessels the *Medway Queen* and *PS Ryde*. The *Medway Queen* was famous for the part she played in evacuating British troops from Dunkirk whilst the *PS Ryde* saw long service on the cross-Solent route from Portsmouth to Ryde. Continue across the second causeway and on reaching the far side follow the riverside north for a further mile until the Folly Inn is reached. Bear to the right of the public house and on joining the access lane turn right and walk up the lane for 200 yards. At the point where Folly Lane swings to the right by the entrance to the caravan park turn left by the footpath sign.

Walk up through the trees and through the two fields and emerge in Beatrice Avenue a short distance beyond Whippingham church. Turn right into Beatrice Avenue and follow the road for ½ mile until it joins the A3021 East Cowes to Newport road. It is well worth

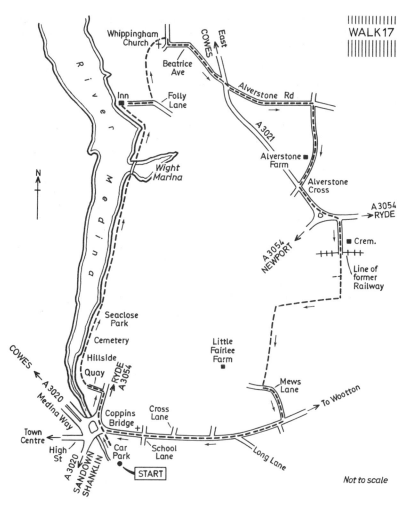

Not to scale

pausing to examine some of the buildings in Whippingham on the way. Opposite the church is a delightful row of ornate, tiled Victorian almshouses whilst the church itself is an imposing Germanic-style structure. The church was designed by the Prince Consort, husband of Queen Victoria, who demolished the previous church (which had been built by John Nash the famous architect who resided at East Cowes Castle) and built the new structure in 1860. Apart from the striking exterior with its tower and spire surrounded by four pinnacles the interior is most ornate. The church contains a number of gifts from Queen Victoria and wall-plaques and gravestones commemorate Prince Louis of Battenburg and

Princess Victoria of Hesse, the parents of the late Earl Mountbatten of Burma. The entrance to the churchyard is by means of a large lych gate of Indian teak.

On reaching the main road cross to the opposite side and turn right. Walk down the path for 100 yards and turn left into Alverstone Road by the Blacksmith's Shop. Walk along Alverstone Road for 600 yards and turn right by the wooded triangle of ground in the road. Continue along this road downhill past the red-brick Alverstone Farm to rejoin the A3021. Turn left uphill and at the top cross to the opposite side by the entrance to Whippingham Crematorium. Walk down the road to the crematorium and cross the old railway line.

From the railway line carry straight on and take the second footpath to the right. This path joins another after 600 yards. Turn left and after 600 yards cross a farm lane. Bear to the left and carry on until the path emerges on the Wootton to Newport Road at Staplers.

Turn right downhill towards Newport. The road offers views over the town towards Carisbrooke and the downs behind Shorwell. Carisbrooke Castle can be seen on its hill in the distance. Staplers Road is pleasantly residential, the Regency Bellecroft House being situated halfway down on the right-hand side. At the bottom of the hill turn left to reach Coppins Roundabout and the entrance to the car park.

Walk 18   Godshill to Rookley

5 miles (8 km)

The countryside between Godshill, Merstone and Rookley provides level walking in a rich agricultural area. This region is bounded by the high downs of Appuldurcombe to the south and the central chalk downs to the north.

The walk starts in Godshill village, where off-street parking is available, and leads north towards Budbridge and Merstone before turning west to Rookley. The return route brings the walker back to Godshill from the Bleakdown area to the west.

From Godshill take the Shanklin direction out of the village past the Griffin Hotel. After 300 yards turn left down the gravelled lane leading to Moor Farm. Walk due north past Moor Farm and cross the farm yard. Continue straight ahead along the track to Great Budbridge Manor turning left to pass to the rear of the buildings after a mile. About 300 yards beyond the manor turn right then left again (westwards) across an open field and the old railway line until the path emerges on the Merstone Road. Bear left along the road and after 300 yards join the A3020 at a place peculiarly named Bohemia.

Turn left up the hill and at the brow turn right up the narrow lane. After 800 yards follow the road to the right to emerge on the Rookley to Chale Green road by the Chequers Inn. The country to the west is known as The Wilderness and the valley is occupied by the upper reaches of the River Medina which originates on St Catherine's Down to the south. Near the summit of St Catherine's Down can be seen a tall obelisk known as Hoy's Monument which was erected by Michael Hoy in honour of a visit by Alexander, Emperor of Russia.

At the road junction by the inn turn back sharp left and follow the narrow lane up the hill. Walk past an old overgrown sandpit on the right and down the other side to Bagwich Farm, an attractive old building on the left side of the road. Turn left just beyond the farm and walk down through the fields crossing the River Yar in the valley.

Walk up the other side to the old railway line. On crossing the track turn right immediately and then left up a lane to join the Whitwell to Godshill road. Cross the road and walk up the road directly opposite. This leads to the centre of Godshill village passing the old church *en route*. After 350 yards turn right up to the church in

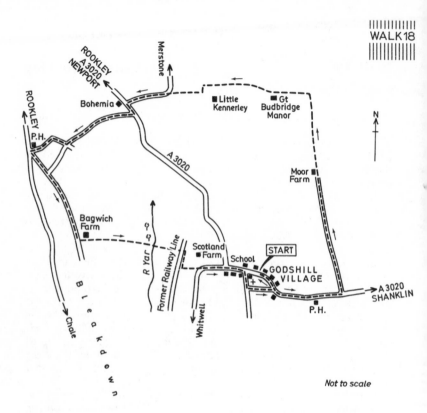

Not to scale

its splendid hilltop setting. On passing Church Hill turn left down past a cottage called Batswing to emerge on the A3020. Cross the road to the footway on the opposite side and walk past an excellent small natural history museum and several thatched gift shops and tea-rooms to the starting point of the walk.

Walk 19   Godshill to Appuldurcombe

5 miles (8 km)

This walk starts in the centre of Godshill village and covers the magnificent farming and downland country to the south. A short excursion off the circular route leads to Gat Cliff which offers superb views of virtually the whole inland Wight, Sandown Bay on the one hand and Freshwater on the other being visible. The route also passes Appuldurcombe House, the ruins of which stand in magnificent parkland. Most of the 5-mile route is gentle walking but there is a steep short climb to Gat Cliff.

The walk starts in Godshill village on the A3020 where parking is available in car parks in the centre of the village.

Leave the car park and walk away from the village and the church towards Shanklin. The Griffin Hotel marks the eastern end of the village, walk past the hotel and after 350 yards turn right up the signposted lane which leads to Freemantle Gate (an old entrance to Appuldurcombe Park). After 400 yards pass the entrance to Godshill Park but continue on the farm lane until the huge stone gate is reached. Enter the field by the path through the right arch and carry on for 150 yards before bearing slightly to the left and crossing the fields diagonally until a small car park is reached below Appuldurcombe House. Step over the stile and turn right up the lane to the house. The entrance is 300 yards up the hill on the left and the house and grounds are well worth visiting.

Appuldurcombe means 'valley of apple trees' and for several hundred years was the seat of the Worsley family. Sir Richard Worsley was the most famous member of the family and his *History of the Isle of Wight* (1781) was one of the earliest accounts of the Island. The house was built in 1710 from a design for Sir Robert by Colin Campbell and was the largest mansion to be built on the Island until the construction of Osborne House. The building is of an unusual design consisting of a three-storey central block with a pedimented wing added to each of its four corners. The main façade of Corinthian pilasters which separate the rows of deep windows are particularly impressive. The house was for many years used as a boys' school and was, for a short period at the turn of the century, occupied by the Benedictine monks who later settled at Quarr Abbey near Ryde.

Return to the entrance to the house and turn right back down the lane. After 100 yards turn left along the footpath which rejoins the

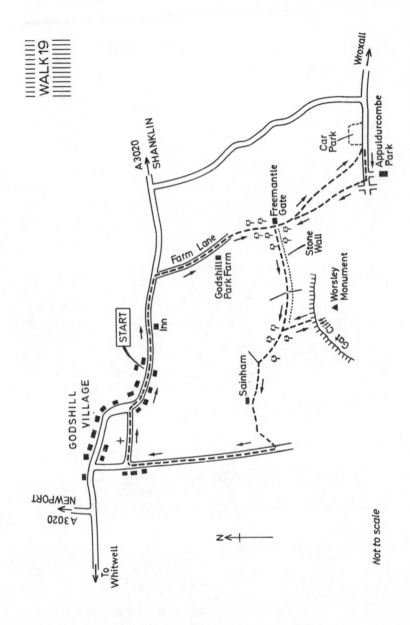

WALK 19

A3020
SHANKLIN

Farm Lane

Godshill
Park Farm

START

Inn

GODSHILL
VILLAGE

A3020
NEWPORT

To
Whitwell

Freemantle
Gate

Stone
Wall

Worsley
Monument

Gat Cliff

Sainham

Car
Park

Appuldurcombe
Park

Wroxall

N

Not to scale

outward route at Freemantle Gate after ½ mile. On reaching the gate turn left up the track through the woods alongside a stone wall until it emerges into a field at the top. Cross this field keeping the stone wall on the left the whole time and follow the path around the foot of Gat Cliff. Where the path enters a copse 200 yards further on turn sharp left up the hill to the summit of Gat Cliff.

As mentioned earlier the views from the summit are outstanding and many of the farms, villages and landmarks, including Godshill church and village, can be seen clearly below. The obelisk was erected by Sir Richard Worsley in 1774 and is constructed of Cornish granite. It was originally some 70 ft in height before it was struck by lightning.

Descend from Gat Cliff by the same route and at the bottom of the Greensand escarpment carry straight on down the hill through the copse and across the fields to Sainham Farm. Just before reaching the farm buildings turn left to emerge, 300 yards later, on a quiet road. Turn right and continue along this road for over ½ mile until the church and adjoining buildings come into view. It is worth walking around the corner to see one of the most photographed of English views, that of Church Hill. Here a picturesque group of thatched cottages lies at the top of a short rising road with the tower of the church behind.

The church site at the top of the hill offers extensive views and is a somewhat unusual situation for such a building. Legend tells that the early inhabitants started to build on level ground about a mile to the south-west. However the following day the labourers found that all the stones had been moved to the top of the hill. Assuming that this was the will of God the new building was recommenced on that site.

The church was built in the fifteenth-century Perpendicular style and is the largest old church on the Island. Part of the church is devoted to the Leigh and Worsley families who inhabited Appuldurcombe in Georgian times and there are a number of tombs to their memory.

Turn right down the lane beside the church to emerge in the centre of Godshill village beside the old cottage called 'Batswing'. This and a number of other cottages in the village have been developed to serve the holiday industry and, although rather commercialized, the character of what must have once been a delightfully peaceful village before the age of the motorcar and tourism remains.

Turn right along the main road past the numerous tea gardens, a good small natural history museum and the Old Smithy to reach the starting point of the walk after about 300 yards.

Walk 20

7½ miles (12 km)

The high downs behind Ventnor provide excellent and energetic walks with splendid sea and inland views. This circular walk commences to the east of Ventnor and covers Bonchurch and St Boniface Downs as well as the ground below the face of the Undercliff between St Lawrence and Ventnor. The walk involves several steep ascents and descents ranging from sea level to nearly 800 feet over a total distance of 7½ miles.

The starting point is at Nansen Hill viewpoint car park on the A3055 Ventnor to Shanklin road just to the Shanklin side of Upper Ventnor adjoining The Landslip.

On leaving the car park cross the main road, step over the stile and follow the sign up the side of the steep down immediately opposite. Walk up the hill for 200 yards, cross a second stile and then turn left and carry on to the summit of Bonchurch Down. The view to the north is most impressive with the village of Luccombe and the National Trust land behind it, and below and beyond the wide sweep of Sandown Bay terminating with the chalk cliffs of Culver. On reaching the hilltop the path is joined by one path from the left and two from the right. Carry straight on at this point with Ventnor and Bonchurch below to the left. Continue past the radar scanners keeping the boundary fence on the right until the path divides then bear left down the steep side of St Boniface Down.

The land to the left is named Bishop's Acre. The name was derived from the tale of a bishop who was riding across the hilltop on a misty night. His horse fell and slipped down towards the cliff edge and the bishop resolved to dedicate an acre of land to St Boniface if he survived. Fortunately the horse caught a hoof in a cleft of a well on the hillside and the bishop survived and was as good as his word.

On descending the side of St Boniface Down look to the right where a hollow in the downs was once the location of Ventnor station, the terminus of the line from Ryde Pier. A long tunnel was cut through the chalk downs to connect the town and the arrival of the railway provided the impetus for the town's rapid expansion in the 1870s. On reaching the bottom of the hill turn left past the Terminus Hotel to join the road. Turn right along Mitchell Avenue and walk up the hill for 400 yards, until the road joins Upper Gills Cliff Road. Turn left here and walk the length of the road until the sharp bend is reached at the western end. Turn right into Whitwell

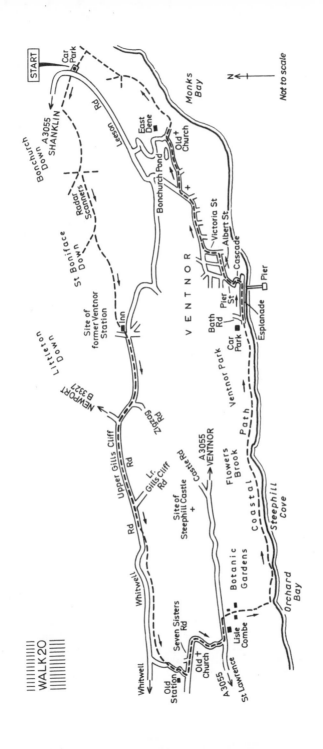

WALK 20

START

Car Park

Bonchurch Down A3055 SHANKLIN

Leeson Rd

East Dene

Monks Bay

Old + Church

Bonchurch Pond

Radar Scanners

St Boniface Down

Littleton Down

Site of former Ventnor Station

Inn

NEWPORT B 3327

Upper Gills Cliff Rd

B 3327 Rd

Lt. Gills Cliff Rd

Castle Rd

Site of Steephill Castle +

A3055 VENTNOR

Whitwell Rd

Seven Sisters Rd

Whitwell

Old Station

Old + Church

A3055

St Lawrence

Lisle Combe

Botanic Gardens

Flowers Brook

Ventnor Park

Car Park

V E N T N O R

Bath Rd

Pier St

Victoria St

Albert St

Cascade

Esplanade

Pier

Coastal Path

Steephill Cove

Orchard Bay

N

Not to scale

Road at this point and after 200 yards join the grass path on the left-hand side of the road. The area of ground in this vicinity is notorious for land movement and large cavities which opened in the road here were of indeterminate depth with the result that a new length of road had to be constructed around them. The cause of this failure was the Gault Clay or 'Blue Slipper' which underlies the chalk and Greensand and becomes most unstable when rain causes ground water to run out over it. The resulting slip plane has caused the land to founder in a belt of destruction running from Bonchurch in the east to Blackgang in the west.

Continue along the path past the end of the housing and the sports ground and the road bears right away from the path after 200 yards. Carry straight on along the cliff edge descending to join St Lawrence Shute after 350 yards. Turn left down the hill over the bridge over the old railway line and turn left into Seven Sisters Road by the old station (see the plaque on the wall of the house). Carry on down the road past St Lawrence old church and several old cottages until A3055 Undercliff Drive is reached.

Turn left alongside the main road and walk through the heavily wooded section past Lisle Combe (on the right) once the home of Alfred Noyes. Turn right off the road 150 yards further on by a wide bend in the road with a large grassed open space. Walk down the steep track past Bank End Farm and continue for 300 yards until the coastal footpath is reached. Turn left following the cliff edge back towards Ventnor. To the left is the Ventnor Botanic Gardens which were once the grounds of the Royal National Hospital for Chest Diseases which was opened in 1868 and closed as recently as 1965. The buildings were demolished and the local council have made an excellent job of extending the grounds, and trees and shrubs flourish in the suntrap position below the sheltered Undercliff.

The demand for medical facilities in the area and indeed the popularity of Ventnor itself arose from the publication in 1830 of a paper by the eminent physician Sir James Clark on 'The influence of climate on health' in which he proclaimed: 'I have seen nothing along the south coast of England that will bear comparison with the Ventnor area.'

Continue along the cliff walk high above Steephill Cove with its sheltered cottages in the bay below and then out onto the open space by Flowers Brook. Inland the hillside is dominated by a number of substantial properties which are situated among the remaining walls of the former Steephill Castle. This castle was built by Sir John Hamborough in 1833 who unfortunately became blind and never saw the completed work. It was eventually demolished some twenty years ago. Sir John was a wealthy benefactor who erected the church and a number of other buildings in Ventnor. After 500 yards the cliff path enters a car park at the western end of Ventnor Esplanade. Pass through the car park and turn right down the hill to the seafront. Walk along the esplanade past the clock tower and bear left up the hill by the drinking fountain outside the pier.

Beneath the winding pedestrian route to the town runs The Cascade, a waterfall which formerly turned a corn mill. Continue up the hill to the top where it joins Pier Street. Walk up Pier Street for 100 yards and turn right into Albert Street. At the top of Albert Street turn left into Victoria Street and then right into High Street. Walk up past the Burts Brewery on the left and the library on the right and then after 300 yards turn right, immediately beyond the church. This road leads into Bonchurch village which contains many attractive Victorian villas and cottages with decorative gables and verandahs, all in a sylvan and rocky setting. Walk past the large pond in the centre of the village and turn right downhill opposite a large crag of rock overhanging the road at the point where the road swings uphill.

During the nineteenth century Bonchurch was much favoured by authors, artists and other famous people. Swinburne, the poet, was buried in the old churchyard and Charles Dickens, Thackeray and Anna Sewell (authoress of *Black Beauty*) also stayed there.

Walk down the lane and bear left after passing the old church and follow the path as it swings to the left. The bay at this point is called Monks Bay after a landing by the monks of Lire to preach their faith to residents of the area. A French invasion force was repulsed here with heavy loss in 1545 when D'Annebauts fleet attempted a landing.

Continue uphill for 400 yards and walk straight on past the point where two paths join from the left. The ground in this area is known as the Landslip where considerable acreages fell away in the eighteenth and nineteenth centuries. After 400 yards turn left and follow the path straight up the hillside to emerge in the corner of Nansen Hill car park, the starting point of this walk.

Walk 21   Bonchurch and the Landslip

3 miles (5 km)

This walk covers the coastline and downland in the vicinity of
Bonchurch and offers a delightful walk through very varied scenery.
The views are far reaching from the highest points of the circular
route. The route covers a distance of 3 miles and starts at sea level
before a steady uphill walk across the Landslip to the Ventnor–
Shanklin road. The next section which leads up to Bonchurch Down
is a strenuous climb but the views reward this. The final length is the
steep descent to Ventnor and back by road to Bonchurch.

Park in Bonchurch village by the pond.

Face the pond then turn right along the road and where a bluff of
rock overhangs the road (where it turns left uphill) turn downhill to
the right. The steep land leads past two large houses, Eastdene on
the left and Winterbourne on the right, before narrowing at
Bonchurch old church. Charles Dickens once stayed at Winterbourne and wrote several chapters of his novels there.

The old church is very small and dates back to Norman times. It
was dedicated to St Boniface who worked in the area in the seventh
century. H. de Vere Stacpoole who wrote *The Blue Lagoon* is buried in
the churchyard. He was just one of the many literary figures who
stayed at Bonchurch. Others include Thackeray, Anna Sewell,
Macauley and, of course, Dickens.

Bear left opposite the church away from the footpath which leads
to the beach and follow the track downhill to the cliff edge. Turn left
at the bottom and follow the cliff path past a farmhouse and then up
a short steep hill before joining the Landslip. This area of broken
ground stretches from this point to Luccombe and has been the site
of several major landslides in the last three centuries. The instability
in this area can be attributed to the underlying Gault Clay or 'Blue
Slipper' which has led to considerable movement in the Ventnor
and Undercliff area.

Continue across the Landslip for 600 yards and take the second
footpath uphill to the left. On joining the second path bear right
again immediately afterwards and walk uphill to emerge on the
A3055 Ventnor to Shanklin road.

Turn right along the road and after 300 yards cross over (opposite
the car park) and enter the field by the stile. Walk straight up the
steep hillside and cross a second stile at the top. Bear left and follow
the path along the top of the down towards Ventnor. After $\frac{3}{4}$ mile

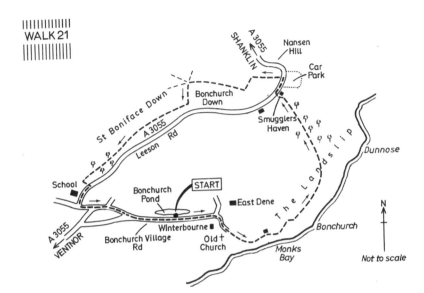

where five paths meet turn left down the side of the hill. Excellent
views of Bonchurch and Ventnor town are to be had from this point.
This path descends very steeply down the south face of Bonchurch
Down. After 350 yards turn right and follow the track along the
400 ft contour eastwards towards Ventnor. After 500 yards the path
enters woodland. Turn sharp left 150 yards further on to join the
A3055 main road behind the school.

Turn right down the hill and at the road junction by the traffic
island turn left. Walk on down the hill and bear left again after 150
yards into Bonchurch village. The return walk through lower
Bonchurch is delightful. The ornate Victorian cottages and villas
with their carved gables and verandahs nestle in a sylvan setting
below the high tree-covered cliffs which shelter the village. Continue
along the village road and return to the starting point by the long
pond which was provided for the village by Stacpoole.

Walk 22

Luccombe to Shanklin

4 miles (6.5 km)

Luccombe lies to the south of Shanklin at the eastern end of the Undercliff and has a long history of land movements over the years.

The walk leads from high ground down to the cliff edge and along the coastal path as far as Shanklin Chine. After descending the chine and returning back up to the Old Village the route passes the old manor and church before the steep uphill walk to Cowleaze and back to Luccombe. The walk involves several steady ascents and descents of steep paths over a total distance of 4 miles.

This walk starts at Nansen Hill viewpoint car park (which adjoins the Landslip) on the A3055 between Ventnor and Shanklin. The car park is on the seaward side of the road at the point where it enters Upper Bonchurch having curved around the downs of Luccombe.

Face the sea and follow the path downhill from the left-hand corner of the car park. After 200 yards this path joins the coastal footpath just before crossing a track. Continue on gently downhill past the ornately thatched Dunnose Cottage on the left to the head of Luccombe Chine. A chine is a local name for a ravine cut in sandstone by a fast flowing stream leading to the sea. Carry on northwards towards Shanklin passing Luccombe village until the road is reached. Walk down the pleasant tree-lined residential road (Luccombe Road) past Shanklin Hospital. After 450 yards by the entrance to Rylstone Gardens bear left down the dark tree-covered path which leads to Shanklin Chine. The walk can be lengthened at this point by turning right after 50 yards through Shanklin Chine which is open to the public. Descend by the winding path through the chine to emerge on the esplanade. Turn left along the esplanade and after 100 yards turn left again up Chine Hill past the Chine Inn. At the top of the hill turn left along Chine Avenue joining the A3055 just above Shanklin Old Village.

It should be noted that there is no public right of way down the chine, but it is well worth the extended walk to see its serene beauty. The stream which carved out the chine passes beneath the road and then forms a waterfall of some 40 ft before following a winding course to the sea. The chine was opened to the public in 1817 by Mr W. Colenutt who built the thatched Fisherman's Cottage which still stands on the beach. As early as 1589 records show that the French collected fresh water from the chine and were ambushed by the English soldiers who were watching from the cliff tops.

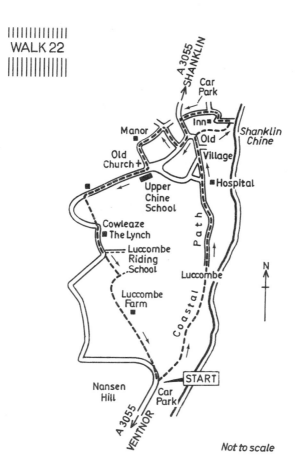

||||||||||||
WALK 22
|||||||||||

A 3055 SHANKLIN

Car Park

Inn

Manor

Old

Shanklin Chine

Old Church +

Village

Upper Chine School

Hospital

Cowleaze
The Lynch

Luccombe Riding School

Path

Luccombe Farm

Luccombe

N

Coastal

START

Nansen Hill

Car Park

A 3055 VENTNOR

Not to scale

This particular part of Shanklin with its shady paths, mossy banks and thatched cottages was much enjoyed by Keats who wrote part of *Endymion* here.

Turn left along the A3055 around the double bend of the Old Village and past the thatched cottages and then right up the narrow lane after 150 yards. Walk up the lane for 200 yards and at the road junction turn left then immediately bear left again. This wide path leads through perhaps the oldest part of Shanklin past the fine old manor to emerge by the pond and old church on the A3055.

On joining the road turn right up the hill past the church and a row of Victorian cottages. After 400 yards turn left opposite the farm up the steep path to the top of Cowleaze Hill. Near the top of the path there are superb views over the towns of Shanklin and Sandown. In the distance can be seen the sandstones of Redcliff and the chalk headland of Culver on the far side of Sandown Bay.

The path reaches the road at the top of the hill. Step over the stile and turn left past 'The Lynch' and over the brow of the hill. A track leads off to the left to Luccombe Riding School after 200 yards. Take the footpath immediately to the right of this (on the bend in the road) down across the fields. After 150 yards the footpath joins a farm track. Turn right for 100 yards and then bear left downhill towards Luccombe Farm which is enclosed in a sheltered fold in the downs. Follow the path around the back of the farm buildings and take a farm track down the hillside to the access road to Dunnose Cottage beside an isolated house. Keeping the house to the left follow the path up the steep slope from the valley to rejoin the A3055. Turn left along the road past the lay-by which offers extensive views over the Landslip to Luccombe beach until Nansen Hill car park is reached 250 yards further on.

Walk 23   Newchurch to Alverstone

3½ miles (5.5 km)

This walk is over the woodland and valley between the central downs and the East Yar. It provides varied walking country with distant downland views as well as a more local variety of woodland, watermeadow and open field.

The walk starts in Newchurch, a quiet village, which lies 2 miles north of the A3056 Newport to Sandown road. Traffic should turn off this road at Branstone Crossroads ½ a mile west of Apse Heath village. The walking is over easy ground and covers about 3½ miles.

Park in the village and face north walking along the village street until School Lane is reached on the right. Turn right down the lane and at the end of the lane turn right across the field. The path bends south and then bears east to join Skinners Lane. Turn left up the lane and at the end by the road junction turn left again along the footpath parallel to the road. Follow the path north across the fields until another road is reached after 600 yards. The wood ahead is Youngwoods Copse and Alverstone Garden Village lies within it. The garden village comprises a small number of select houses in the beautiful sylvan setting and a short walk to the left here leads into the village. After visiting the village return to this point and cross the lane and enter the narrow track through the woods. This path follows the eastern edge of Youngwoods Copse and then joins a gravel road which bears right to join the Alverstone village road. Turn left down the hill passing the old station on the left and then by a stone wall step over the stile on the left to follow the bank of the Yar inland from the village. Walk along the path bounded by shrubs on both sides. To the left is Alverstone Mill which has for some time been a private residence. Continue across the weir and walk along the river bank on the far side. After 400 yards bear left away from the river and cross the railway line. Walk uphill for 200 yards and then bear right circuiting a small hill until the track divides. Turn right at this junction and carry on for 300 yards. This path leads back towards Newchurch village. At the next junction turn right and follow the path along the edge of a coppice. After 400 yards turn left and emerge in Newchurch village by the church.

Although the name of this village suggests modernity the name derives from Norman times. The church with its wooden tower is particularly attractive in its hilltop location. The view from this end of the village is far reaching with farms and contrasting farmland

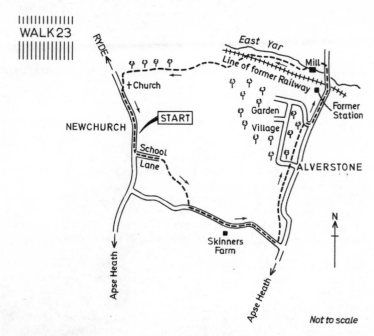

making a rich pattern against the backcloth of the chalk downs to the north. Turn back, away from the church, along the village street to reach the starting point of the walk.

Walk 24   Arreton to Newchurch

6 miles (9.5 km)

The Arreton Valley comprises the richest farmland to be found on the Isle of Wight, the sandy soils and sunny sheltered position being ideally suited for market gardening and cereal production. The countryside consists of undulating fields backed by the high chalk downs and is varied walking country.

This walk starts at Arreton where parking can be found by the church behind the White Lion public house on the A3056 Newport to Sandown road. The walk is approximately 6 miles in length and over even country with the exception of a short ascent and descent over the downs near the mid-point and end of the route.

Walk down the lane from the church past some old stone cottages and join the A3056 by the White Lion pub. Turn left along the main road and after 100 yards bear left behind Arreton School. Continue along the lane and across the fields passing a north-south path after ½ mile. To the right is Heasley Manor, a fine rambling old building which is open to the public and is in the process of being restored. Keep the hedge on the right until the path joins a narrow lane with hedges on both sides. After 200 yards join the Newchurch to Mersley Down Road.

Turn left up the road and after 100 yards cross the road and turn right into the field. Turn right again after 75 yards and continue until the path re-emerges on the road below Knighton Farm. Turn left up the road walking past the old stone gates of the former Knighton Manor and up the hill to join the 'downs road'. Turn left along the downs road, on reaching the top of the hill pause to examine the panoramic view to the south. To the left the church of Newchurch can be seen on the top of its hill whilst Sandown Bay and Dunnose headland is beyond. The high downs due south are those behind Ventnor with St Catherine's Hill to the right. The patchwork of ploughed fields and small woodlands forms a delightful contrast to the green backcloth of the chalk downs.

Continue westwards along the downs road for 1¾ miles. The views are excellent and far reaching to the north and south and this section of the walk offers a fine appreciation of the Island's landscape and geological structure.

Walk past the road junction on the left which leads down the side of the hill to Mersley Farm and take the second path signposted to Arreton on the left (the first path leads straight down to Heasley

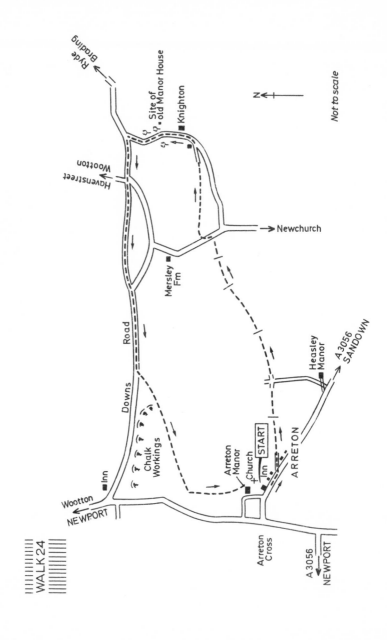

WALK 24

Manor). The path descends gradually, passing a large chalk quarry on the right. Turn left after 300 yards and continue straight down the hill to the group of buildings in the trees below.

The old village of Arreton through which this path now passes forms a fine group of historic buildings. The manor (which is open to the public) was built in the Jacobean style by Sir Levinus Bennet and a date over the central porch reads 1639. The plan of the manor is that of the letter 'H' with two projecting gables, one on each side of the porch. The interior is well decorated with fine wood panelling and carved chimney pieces and now houses a museum.

Proceeding down the path, the remains of the old tithe barn can be seen while on the right is the old church. This building represents the change from Norman to early English style and dates from the eleventh century. The church was much improved in the thirteenth century by the monks of Quarr Abbey (near Binstead) to whom the tithes were handed in 1140. The dominant features are the huge buttresses which were added to support the tower after it was struck by lightning in 1481.

At the north-east end of the church the grave of Elizabeth Wallbridge, known locally as 'The Dairyman's Daughter', can be found. She was immortalized in the book by Rev Legh Richmond (Vicar of Brading) *Annals of the Poor* which had a world-wide circulation at the beginning of the nineteenth century.

Emerge from the footpath by the church to join the lane behind the White Lion at the starting point of the walk.

Walk 25   Ryde to Wootton

8 miles (13 km)

The town of Ryde is the starting point of this walk and the route leads through some of the fine streets of Victorian seaside villas to the outskirts and the villages of Binstead and Wootton beyond. The return walk covers woodland, farmland and residential roads. The total length of the walk is 8 miles with gentle gradients.

The starting point is St Thomas' Street which leads from the western end of Ryde Esplanade where there are two public car parks.

Turn uphill on leaving the car park past the imposing Brigstocke Terrace which has been recently restored and which backs onto the Royal Victoria Arcade. Turn right into Spencer Road and walk along its whole length past the junction with West Street and then past the marine villa Westfield Park. Follow on to the gravelled narrow lane and then bear left to emerge by the entrance to Ryde Golf Course. At the main road turn right into Ladies Walk which leads alongside the course. This was a particularly popular walk in Victorian times with ladies strolling from their villas in Spencer Road westward through the woodlands to Binstead church.

Delightful views of the Solent can be gained from this walk. The name Solent is allegedly derived from the Latin word *Solveo* to loosen, and refers to the separation of the Island from mainland England by natural causes. On reaching the far side of the golf course enter the woods and follow the surfaced path down to the stream. Cross the small bridge and walk uphill until Binstead church is reached. The church has a late thirteenth-century chancel but unfortunately the building was badly damaged by a fire in 1969.

Turn left along the road and then bear right almost immediately and follow the road round the double bend. Where the road straightens take the path to the right through the woods to Quarr. After 400 yards the path emerges into the sylvan setting of the residential Quarr Road. Turn right along the road until the gate is reached at the end. Continue downhill along the well-defined track to pass eventually under an old stone archway near the old Quarr Abbey. A short distance ahead to the right can be seen the tall pink spire of the newer abbey building rising from the trees.

To the right of the path lie the old abbey ruins of 'Our Lady of the Quarry'. Few of the buildings can now be seen with only a boundary wall and one of the large fishponds remaining. In its time this abbey

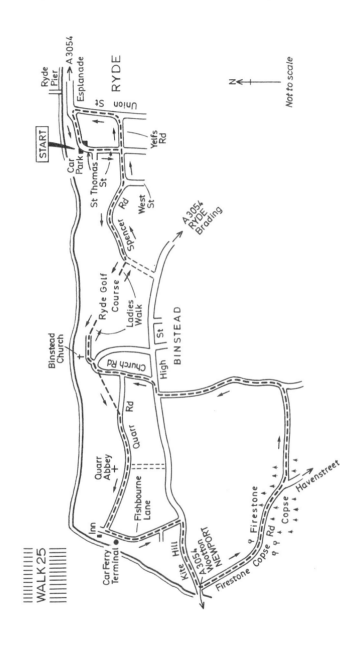

WALK 25

RYDE

Ryde Pier
A3054
Esplanade
Union St
START
Car Park
St Thomas St
Yelfs Rd
Spencer Rd
West St
A3054 RYDE Brading
Ryde Golf Course
Ladies Walk
BINSTEAD
High St
Binstead Church
Church Rd
Quarr Rd
Quarr Abbey
Fishbourne Lane
Inn
Car Ferry Terminal
Kite Hill
A3054 Wootton NEWPORT
Firestone Copse Rd
Firestone Copse
Havenstreet

N

Not to scale

was the most important on the Island with great wealth in the form of land and property. The abbey was founded in 1132 by Baldwin de Redvers, Lord of the Isle of Wight. The stone for the building was obtained from the one-time famous but now long-defunct Binstead Quarries. Stone from these quarries was sent to the mainland for the construction of the cathedrals of Chichester and Winchester and for Winchester College.

In 1550 on the dissolution of the monastries the property was purchased for demolition and the stone was sold for the construction of Henry VIII's coastal defences at Yarmouth and Cowes. In about 1900 some monks from Solesmes in France came to Appuldurcombe and they started the rebuilding of the new abbey in 1907. The rose pink coloured Flemish bricks were imported and the effect is pleasing.

Continue up the gravel road and 250 yards beyond the archway cross the main drive to the new abbey. Enter the woodland path opposite which later reverts to a private gravel roadway eventually joining Fishbourne Lane. Turn left up the road past the Sealink ferry terminal until the A3054 Ryde to Newport road is reached. Cross by the traffic island and turn right along Kite Hill past a pleasant row of large Sussex-farmhouse-style properties. Turn left 300 yards beyond the brow of the hill into Firestone Copse Road. This road leads through Forestry Commission land and then swings eastwards to Binstead village. On entering the wooded section of roadway continue for about 400 yards then take the road to the left a short distance after a sharp bend. Continue on this road for just under a mile passing Newnham Farm on the right. Turn left at the farm and then right again after 200 yards to Bartletts Corner at the southern end of the residential Newnham Road. Turn left along Newnham Road and walk to the end where it joins A3054 Binstead Hill. Cross the main road and walk straight ahead down Church Road which leads past Binstead church which was encountered on the outward journey. Turn right by the church down the path and back across Ryde Golf Course by Ladies Walk. Turn left on leaving this path down into Spencer Road. At the Ryde end of the road cross St Thomas' Street into the quiet close (Yelfs Road) which is a cul-de-sac for vehicles. At the far end walk between the posts and turn left down the fine wide Union Street, the main shopping area and thoroughfare. Pause to look up and examine the architecture. Ryde is one of fifty-four towns in Britain which is noted as being of particular interest for its Victorian architecture. A few paces downhill on the left is the Royal Victorian Arcade which has enjoyed an active life since its restoration.

Walk to the bottom of Union Street and turn left onto the esplanade. The dominant feature is the pier which was opened in 1824 and is $\frac{1}{2}$ mile in length. Unlike many similar structures in other resorts this pier plays an active role in the Island's tourist industry and communications network with passengers arriving by ferry at the Pier Head and trains running from there to Ryde Esplanade, Brading, Sandown and Shanklin. Proceed along the esplanade for 100 yards and bear left into St Thomas' Street where the car parks will be reached after a short distance.

Walk 26   Seaview to Ryde

6 miles (9.5 km)

This route covers the north-east corner of the Island between
Seaview and Ryde and comprises coastal and inland footpaths. The
walk starts in the centre of the unspoilt village of Seaview which lies
a short distance off the B3330 road from Ryde to St Helens and
Bembridge. The first part of the route follows the sea-wall from
Seaview to Ryde with views of Solent shipping, and on reaching
Ryde it turns inland through the rural areas of Bullen and Pondwell.
The return route follows wooded paths and village streets back to
Seaview. The walking is easy and covers a total distance of 6 miles.

Unrestricted parking can be found in many of the side streets of
Seaview off the High Street as there is no public car park nearby.

From the parking place walk to the High Street and proceed down
the hill to the seafront. Turn left along the esplanade and at the end
bear left then carry straight ahead along Bluett Avenue. Turn right,
back towards the sea, opposite the row of old salt workers' cottages
facing the road. Turn left along the old toll road towards Ryde. This
walk offers superb views across the Solent to Portsmouth and
Southsea.

Seaview and Ryde to the west have always been popular for
bathing and Seagrove Bay a short distance from Seaview was
particularly popular at the turn of the century and has retained its
popularity to this day.

Continue along the toll road and at the far end follow the road
past fine villas and boarding houses for a further 400 yards until the
road bends sharply to the left. At this point carry straight on along
the footpath along the sea-wall. On the landward side of the path is
the remains of Puckpool Battery (one of a string of massive defences
constructed on the Island's north coast) which is now a pleasure
garden. After 800 yards the path joins the eastern end of Ryde
Esplanade. The grounds on the left were formerly occupied by fine
marine villas which were demolished to make way for new
development and which were well illustrated by the early engravers
Barber, Cooke and Brannon.

On reaching Ryde Esplanade turn left immediately up the narrow
road leading through Appley Park. Carry on straight up the hill and
join the Ryde–Brading road (A3055) by a small Victorian lodge
which was once the entranceway to Appley House. Cross the road
and walk straight ahead along the residential Marlborough Road.

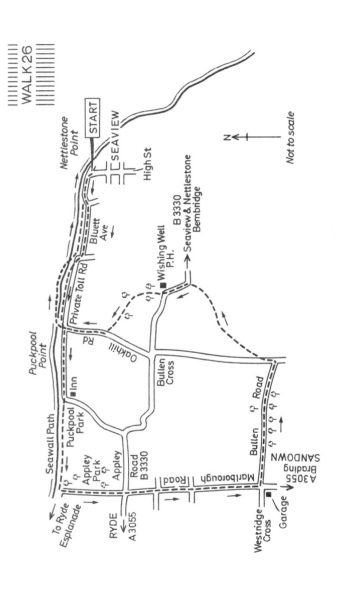

WALK 26

START

Nettlestone
Point

SEAVIEW

High St

Wishing Well
P.H.

B 3330
Seaview & Nettlestone
Bembridge

Bluett
Ave

Private Toll Rd

Oakhill
Rd

Bullen
Cross

Puckpool
Point

Inn

Puckpool
Park

Seawall Path

Appley
Park

Appley
Road
B 3330

Marlborough Road

Bullen Road

A3055
Brading
SANDOWN

To Ryde
Esplanade

RYDE
A3055

Westridge
Cross

Garage

N

Not to scale

Continue for ½ mile and at Westridge Cross by the filling station turn left into Bullen Road.

Walk along Bullen Road past some large houses and down a dip in the road where it enters woodland and then rise up the other side. After 500 yards the road bends sharply to the left. Turn left here and after 100 yards turn right onto the footpath which leads downhill to Pondwell. This path joins a second path after 200 yards and you carry on downhill at this point to emerge on the bend at Pondwell Hill. Turn left along the road for 300 yards and then cross over by The Wishing Well public house. To the left-hand side of the pub a path leads back to the sea. Follow this path downhill until it joins the shady Oakhill Road.

Turn right down Oakhill Road, walk past the entrance to Puckpool Park and rejoin the seafront road by the Battery Hotel. Turn right again back along the seafront to Seaview. Out at sea the forts known as Palmerston Follies can be seen clearly. These massive buildings are known as Spitbank, No Mans Land, St Helens Fort and Horse Sand Fort. These were constructed on the instruction of Lord Palmerston between 1860 and 1880 as a deterrant against a possible invasion by the French. Some three hundred years earlier the French had mounted an unsuccessful invasion of the Island near Seaview.

The method of construction of the forts was advanced for the time, the concrete footings being floated into position and then the massive granite blocks built up. The forts are honeycombed with passages and were able to house a huge garrison. Attempts to demolish them have been fruitless with more structural damage resulting to the properties ashore.

After reaching the end of the esplanade walk along the toll road and back into Seaview village via the outward route along Bluett Avenue.

The village of St Helens which is situated above Brading Harbour at the mouth of the East Yar provides the starting point of this walk and has historical associations which will be described later. This walk leads down from the village to the harbour and over a causeway to a wild area of sand dunes called The Duver. The route swings north through woodland and fields towards the popular Seagrove Bay before returning to St Helens via Nettlestone. The gradients are gentle and comprise an easy walk of 5 miles.

St Helens is a pleasant village on the Ryde to Bembridge road and parking is available in the centre by the Green.

Turn out of the car park or walk from Upper Green Road down across the green to Lower Green Road. Turn left along the road and take the third turning to the right which is a narrow surfaced lane leading down to a caravan site. Walk down the lane rounding the bend at the bottom and on reaching a fine stone house (the converted St Helens Mill) turn left along a concrete wharf. At the harbour end of the wharf a large sign directs pedestrians to the left. The path now continues across a causeway over the harbour with splendid views of the yachting to the right and an opportunity to observe the marsh and heathland birds of the area.

On reaching the far side of the Causeway the path enters the gorse and rough grass which covers The Duver. The Duver is renowned for its flora and over 260 species have been recorded on this National Trust land. Some of the plants of particular interest include the yellow and white stoneworts, tree lupins, green mouse-ear and the blue flowered autumn squill. In its sandy soil such species as sea holly and sea beet can be found. Turn right here and walk towards the buildings visible ahead on the spit. On joining the narrow access road turn left and walk for $\frac{1}{2}$ mile until it joins Eddington Road by a small stone house. To the right on the harbour shore is the old St Helens church which was built in the twelfth century. The stones from the building were found to be particularly effective for scrubbing the decks of wooden ships and were known as Holystones. As a result of coastal erosion only the tower of the church now remains.

Cross the road and enter the field opposite walking gently uphill for 300 yards then bear right slightly until the access lane to the holiday camp is reached. Turn right along the drive and then bear

91

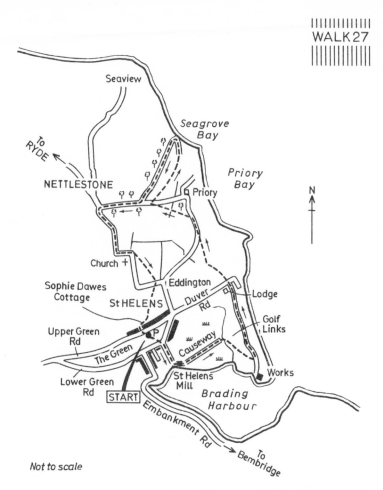

Not to scale

off to the left after 200 yards. Turn right after 300 yards and walk on until the houses are reached by the access point to Seagrove Bay. This bay was a particularly popular bathing beach at the turn of the century and retains its popularity today.

Turn left and follow the road round the bend and straight ahead for 600 yards. On reaching a minor junction turn right and walk uphill until the main road is reached in Nettlestone village. Turn left through this straggling village which backs onto open farmland and follow the road round the sharp left-hand bend by the church 400 yards ahead. Walk on with the churchyard wall on the right and at the next sharp bend enter the field straight ahead. (In wet weather the way out of this field can be muddy so continue along the road for

500 yards.) Walk diagonally across the field to rejoin the St Helens road having thus bypassed a bend in the road.

Cross over the road and enter a confined path which emerges about halfway along Upper Green Road, St Helens, 600 yards later. Turn left along the road and after a short distance an old cottage with shutters and a wall plaque will be seen. This cottage was the home of Sophie Dawes, 'Queen of Chantilly' (born 1792) who was perhaps one of the most notorious of Island residents. She grew up in St Helens, being the daughter of Dicky Dawes a renowned smuggler and shell fisherman. After a period in a workhouse Sophie was, on account of her good looks, later rescued from a brothel by an aide to the Duc de Bourbon whose mistress she became. After a number of years with the exiled Duc the opportunity came in 1814 for him to return to France and he hoped to leave Sophie behind. Sophie however followed him and soon discovered that he had inherited vast fortunes on the death of his father. The aging Duc was soon aware of Sophie's motives and he feared for his life. Shortly afterwards the Duc died in mysterious circumstances; it appeared that he had committed suicide by hanging.

Sophie escaped trial and a murder charge only by the intervention of the King of France and she returned to England shortly afterwards with a vast fortune. After purchasing an estate in Hampshire she gave all the outstanding money to charity, perhaps out of a feeling of guilt. Three years later Sophie died of a heart attack, escaping the discovery of her murderous exploits which were revealed a short while later.

From Upper Green Road turn back to the parking area close to the centre of the green where the walk started.

Walk 28   Brading to Nunwell
3½ miles (5.5 km)

The length of the central downland ridge which runs between Brading in the east and Newport to the west is a natural vantage point for those motorists using the 'downs road'. The views of the fertile Arreton Valley to the north with the high downs of the South Wight behind are remarkable for the extent of the vista and the variety of colour of soil, crop and vegetation. A favourite viewpoint is at the eastern end of this road ½ mile uphill from Brading where parking is available on the north side of the road overlooking Sandown and Sandown Bay beyond.

The route descends part of the south side of the down before swinging east and north through Brading. The return route borders the historic Nunwell Estate before rising up the north side of the downs to return to the car park. The walk is easy walking over a total distance of 3½ miles.

The starting point can be reached by turning uphill at the traffic signals at Yarbridge Cross, Brading, or by travelling along the downs road from Newport. Parking is restricted to certain parts of Brading Down by rustic fencing and access points in between can be seen clearly.

Park on the south side of the road and walk to the road edge then turn right down the hill towards Brading. After 400 yards turn right along a chalk track which leads past a chalk quarry and soon emerges on the minor road to Adgestone below. On reaching the road turn right and walk downhill. Turn left off the road after 250 yards just before a cottage is reached and walk across the field until it joins the Lower Adgestone Road. Turn left passing several cottages on the left-hand side. After 300 yards a sign will be seen showing a pedestrian route to Brading Roman Villa to the right. Walk up the steps and after 200 yards the Roman villa will be passed on the right. This villa was discovered in 1880 and must be considered as one of the major archaeological finds in southern England. The plan of the villa was a number of rooms arranged around a courtyard, with a corridor of rooms forming a residential area in the centre of the building. Perhaps the most impressive feature of this villa is the elaborate mosaic decorations which are exposed in four of the floor areas; hypocausts have also been found in a number of the rooms. The villa buildings on this site were very extensive and their area ran to thousands of square feet; many coins

Not to scale

including silver denarii have been found in the area. Apart from coinage other articles recovered from the site include pottery, glass vases, ornaments and bronze jewellery and iron tools.

It is difficult to put an exact date on this villa but it is likely that it was occupied about 200 AD, and its situation at the eastern end of an old highway which ran from Freshwater to Brading Harbour may be relevant in deducing the importance and functions of its owner. The villa is open to the public and is well worth visiting.

After passing the villa continue down the access lane to the road junction. Turn left along the road (passing Morton Manor after 400 yards) until a road junction is reached. Bear right here then take the second left turning on meeting the main road which leads to Yarbridge Crossroads on the right and the downs to the left.

Walk up the hill and pass the downs road turning to the left after 300 yards. Continue on past some pleasant villas and cottages which have outstanding views eastwards over the meandering River Yar in its wide valley. As the road descends a row of terraced cottages will be passed on the left and a lane leads up the side of these. A short distance up the lane on the right can be seen Little Jane's Cottage a charming small thatched cottage.

Little Jane's Cottage is an eyebrowed cottage, built in 1547, and is famous for its association with the Reverend Legh Richmond of Brading. The Rev Richmond wrote a book entitled *Annals of the Poor* which achieved enormous sales in the last century. One story told of Little Jane the Cottager who was cared for by the vicar during a serious illness but unfortunately she died of tuberculosis at an early age. Richmond's book was successful because of his vivid and perceptive descriptions of the lives of country people and the poor of the Island.

Walk on downhill until the A3055 is reached at Brading High Street. Continue downhill past the Bullring and through the High Street. Pass the wax museum and town hall (with stocks and whipping post) and turn left into Coach Lane 250 yards beyond the church.

After 450 yards the main entrance to Nunwell House is passed. Turn left after 75 yards along a path which follows the north boundary of Nunwell Estate. This path continues straight ahead for nearly a mile until the lane to Nunwell Farm is joined. Turn left along the lane past the farm and at Nunwell West Lodge turn right keeping the copse on the left. At the point where this path meets an east-west path turn left and then after 200 yards bear right uphill until the Brading Down road is reached. Turn left along the road and the starting point of the walk will be reached after 400 yards.

Walk 29   Yaverland to Brading

7 miles (11 km)

The high chalk downs at the eastern end of the Island offer interesting walks with panoramic views over the low-lying land to the north and south. This particular route is over varied countryside and is for the most part easy walking with a steady gradient over the first mile.

The walk starts at Yaverland car park at the far eastern end of Sandown Esplanade opposite Sandown Zoo and leads up onto Culver Down where the whole of the north-east Wight and mainland beyond is laid out below like a map. The route descends the north slope of the down and crosses the flood plain of the meandering East Yar river to Brading. The return route is across farmland and through Yaverland village.

Having parked at Yaverland, face the sea and turn left to the point where the edge of the car park meets the downs. A well-worn track can be seen for the next mile following the cliff edge to the summit of Culver Down where a large stone obelisk is clearly visible. Keep to the cliff path for ¾ mile past the yellow-brown clays and the 'Redcliff' of ferruginous sandstone onto the chalk. The clay cliffs below have yielded many dinosaur remains and are the oldest rocks to be found on the Island. (Many of the relics are displayed in the Museum of Isle of Wight Geology which is situated above Sandown Library.) The transition from the sandstone to chalk will be detected by botanists by the change in vegetation from gorse to the short grass of the chalk downland. A short distance onto the chalk downs and the path swings inland directly to the monument. After 300 yards the path joins the road which runs to the extremity of Culver Cliff 450 yards to the right. Cross the road and pass through the gate to the monument.

Culver Down probably derives its name from the Saxon word 'Culfre' (a dove). The cliff was more famous, however, for a particular breed of falcon. This species was in such demand that in 1564 Queen Elizabeth I directed Sir Richard Worsley, the Island's governor, 'to make diligent search' after some had been stolen. The monument on the summit of the down is known as the Yarborough Obelisk after the first earl who was the founder of the Royal Yacht Squadron. Formerly the monument stood a few hundred yards to the west but the construction of the fort caused it to be resited.

From the monument bear right northwards towards Whitecliff

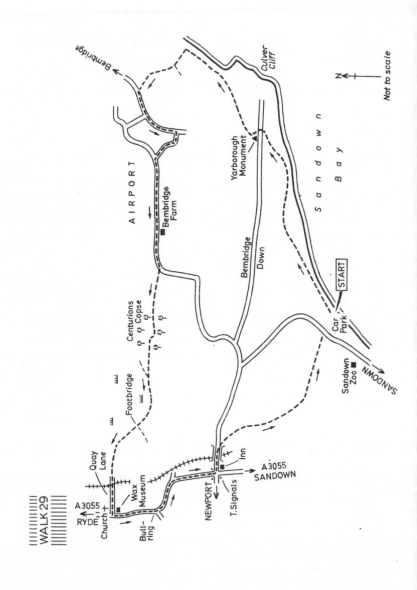

WALK 29

Bembridge

AIRPORT

Bembridge Farm

Centurions Copse

Footbridge

Quay Lane

Wax Museum

A3055
RYDE

Church

Bull-ring

NEWPORT

T. Signals

Inn

A3055
SANDOWN

Bembridge Down

Yarborough Monument

Culver Cliff

Sandown Bay

START

Car Park

Sandown Zoo

SANDOWN

N

Not to scale

Bay below. After 200 yards turn right off the down onto the fenced footpath which leads down to the cliff edge. Walk along the top of the cliffs above Whitecliff Bay turning left inland at the signed path after 800 yards. Continue for 100 yards and bear right at the fork until the path joins the Brading to Bembridge road. Turn left along the road, walk past Bembridge Airport on the right and where the road bends to the left (600 yards beyond the airport entrance) carry straight ahead down the track through the woods to the River Yar.

The path crosses Centurion's Copse which was named after St Urian and converges with a second path from the right 200 yards after leaving the copse. Continue across the valley towards Brading for 200 yards and at the point where two more footpaths join the trail turn right over the footbridge across the river. Carry straight on until the path joins the end of Quay Lane by the sewage treatment works. The lane now leads westwards to the centre of Brading village and was once the main access route to the harbour. The Yar Valley was once a large and sheltered haven for vessels but its importance declined with the silting up of the harbour. Until as recently as 1880 the harbour was in use but the construction of an embankment at the river mouth caused this to cease with the subsequent reclaiming of the rich alluvial pastures for agriculture.

After 700 yards Quay Lane joins the A3055 at High Street and there are several local buildings of importance in the immediate vicinity. On the right-hand junction is the old town hall with its stocks and whipping post and the church behind. Brading church has a chapel dedicated to the Oglander family of nearby Nunwell House whose direct ancestor came to the Island with the Norman Conquest. In addition the church bears a plaque in memory of Rev Legh Richmond who was curate in charge from 1797–1805. His book *Annals of the Poor* told stories of the poor people of the Island and was translated into many languages. On the left-hand corner of this junction is Osborn-Smith's Wax Museum which is contained in, reputedly, the oldest house on the Island. The house was built about 1499 and is the sole surviving Tudor-framed building on the Island. It was a coaching inn haunted by sailors and smugglers from the harbour in Elizabethan and Jacobean times. It now contains excellent wax tableaux depicting many local figures.

Turn left down the High Street and then up the hill. On the central traffic island at the top of the High Street is the Bullring which was formerly used for bull baiting. Turn left at this point and follow the main road round the bend to the right out of Brading. Continue for 600 yards until the traffic light junction is reached by the Anglers Inn. Turn left down the road and across the bridge over the railway line. After 150 yards turn right down the path that leads south-eastwards across the Yar Valley towards Yaverland. Continue for $\frac{1}{2}$ mile and then bear left for a further $\frac{1}{2}$ mile until the path emerges on the Bembridge to Sandown road.

For a glimpse of perhaps the finest of the Island's Jacobean manor-houses turn left along the road for 500 yards. Yaverland Manor was built in 1620 on the site of a previous building which was owned by the Russell family. Sir Theobold died fighting the French when they attacked the Island nearby in 1340. The small twelfth-century church close by forms a most attractive group with the mullioned and gabled old manor-house. Turn back along the road until it rejoins Sandown Esplanade.

Turn left off the esplanade into the car park entrance to complete the walk.

Walk 30

Culver to Bembridge

6 miles (9 km)

This walk covers the high chalk downs and cliffs at the extreme eastern end of the Island close to Culver. The path starts on the summit of the down and follows the coastal path northwards with a return walk through woodland and farmland. The circular route covers a total distance of 6 miles of gentle walking.

The starting point is the Earl of Yarborough's monument on the summit of Culver Down. Turn off the Sandown to Bembridge road ½ mile north of Yaverland and drive up the steep hill to the far end of the down. Pass the old fort and park on the grassy downland beyond.

Turn left and walk along the lane towards the monument. Enter the field to the left immediately in front of the monument and then bear right down the hill. After 150 yards join the fenced-in footpath which leads down towards the cliff edge above Whitecliff Bay. To the north there are splendid views of the country between Bembridge and Ryde with the Haven clearly visible. In the foreground can be seen Bembridge Airport where the highly successful Islander aircraft was developed.

Continue along the path above Whitecliff Bay. To the right can be seen the high chalk cliffs whilst immediately below are the coloured sands and clays of the Tertiary era of geological time which are similarly displayed at Alum Bay at the western end of the Island. Follow the cliff edge for nearly 2 miles and turn left inland by the Crab and Lobster Hotel and the coastguard station.

Follow the lane up behind and to the right of the hotel until it joins Foreland Fields. Turn left and after 200 yards turn right again into Egerton Road. At the end of the road turn left into Lane End Road. Walk along Lane End Road for 300 yards and at the junction carry straight on past the Birdham Hotel turning right at Steyne Crossroads 800 yards later just before a large chalk-stone barn.

Walk along the road for 400 yards and on the left can be seen the sails of Bembridge Windmill. Turn left up the lane leading to the windmill and walk past it after noting that it is the last remaining windmill on the Island. The mill was restored by enthusiasts and is now in the ownership of the National Trust who open it to the public. Continue along the track until it enters Steyne Copse. Carry on through the trees to emerge on the Bembridge to Brading road just east of Bembridge Airport. Walk along the main road past the

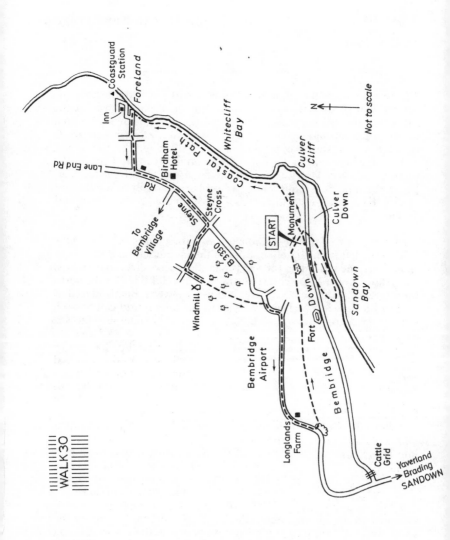

WALK 30

Coastguard Station
Foreland
Inn
Whitecliff Bay
Coastal Path
Lane End Rd
Birdham Hotel
Rd
Steyne
Steyne Cross
To Bembridge Village
B3330
START
Monument
Culver Cliff
Culver Down
Windmill
Sandown Bay
Fort Down
Bembridge Airport
Bembridge
Longlands Farm
Cattle Grid
Yaverland
Brading
SANDOWN

N
Not to scale

airport entrance and then past Bembridge Farm. Follow the road round a sharp left-hand bend and 300 yards beyond the thatched Longlands Farm turn left off the corner by an old chalk quarry. Follow the path along the base of the down for $\frac{1}{2}$ mile and then bear right gently uphill until a second old quarry is reached. Walk straight ahead to the far side of the quarry and then bear right diagonally up the side of the down until the path emerges at the Earl of Yarborough's monument.

Walk past the monument into the lane and cross over into the field opposite and follow the path down to the cliff edge. By contrast to the northern view the vista in this direction is of high cliffs and the wide sweep of Sandown Bay. The high downs between Shanklin and Ventnor can be seen in the distance with Dunnose Point (the eastern end of the Undercliff) jutting into the sea.

Continue along the cliff edge for 400 yards and then turn sharp right following the path back uphill to rejoin the lane by the monument. On reaching the lane turn left to return to the starting point.